"When People Were Nice and Things Were Pretty"

A Culinary History of Merigold:

a Mississippi Delta Town

By

Renelda Owen

Foreword

As I was researching the culinary history of Merigold, Sue Latham told me about a conversation she had with a childhood friend. As they recalled memories of their youth, the friend said, "Aren't you glad we grew up when things were pretty and people were nice?" That comment has come to my mind frequently as I have compiled this book. It seemed to capture the essence of what Merigold culture has been like throughout its history—with an appreciation of the niceities of gentle society that have too often gone by the wayside in our rushed instant access existence today. This book explores a time and place that valued making everyday events such as a noon meal at home or a community potluck be both "pretty and nice," and celebrates those who continue that tradition as it was passed to them by their mothers and grandmothers.

This book is a labor of love for the remarkable people of Merigold United Methodist Church and its surrounding community. Merigold has a fascinating history and is a microcosm of many Mississippi Delta towns and of small southern towns beyond the Delta. The primary documents to which I was given access give an interesting glimpse into the mealtime habits of Merigold throughout its first century. The candid and always entertaining interviews granted to me in preparation of this book gave me a more in depth understanding of the town and its history, and for each person who answered my questions and shared their recolletions, I am deeply grateful.

Because of the uniqueness of the primary documents used to compile this cookbook, it is in a sense, three cookbooks in one: historic recipes from the 1920s and the 1950s, and a current collection of favorite recipes from today's cooks in Merigold. I have chosen to present the archival recipes grouped chronologically, in order to capture a sense of the time and place in which these recipes were enjoyed. I have retained their unique ways of describing amounts and ingredients, and even their variations in spelling, such as the prevailing use of "cocoanut" rather than "coconut" in the 1922 collection. The recipes from today's cooks are presented in the traditional categories one would normally find in a cookbook. For your convenience, there is a categorized index at the back of this book to help you access the treasure trove of recipes contained throughout this volume from the nearly one century of good eating compiled here. Most of all, in the tradition of Granny Millard's reading the cookbook to her little charges instead of bedtime stories in William Faulkner's *The Unvanquished*, I hope you find delicious delight in savoring the reading of these historic recipes and the stories that go with them.

Table of Contents

The front cover photograph was made in Mrs. Edgar (Bess) Rayner's living room in Merigold at a Monday afternoon meeting of the United Methodist Women. Seated from left to right are Mrs. Alice Latham, Mrs. G. C. (Thyra) Richardson, and Mrs. T. R. (Edna Lawrence) Park.

Why Merigold?

The first time I can remember hearing of Merigold, Mississippi was when I was introduced to McCarty Pottery while I was living as a newlywed on the other side of the state. I fell in love with the hand formed pottery that was then available at the Calico Mushroom in New Albany. It became for me the gold standard for judging beautiful ceramic vessels. I knew it was made in a place called Merigold, Mississippi, but I had no idea at that time where Merigold was. Seven years ago my family and I moved to the Mississippi Delta when my husband became pastor of nearby Cleveland First United Methodist Church and of Merigold United Methodist Church, while I began teaching English at Delta State University. I soon became fascinated with Merigold, its vast, flat, rich alluvial land, its history, and its people.

As I have lived and worked in the Mississippi Delta, I have learned that there are several things connected to Merigold that are known around the country, from unusual restaurants to a fabled juke joint; from an art gallery to a historic hunting club; all from a small town with a population of only 662 as of the 2000 U. S Census. Of course there is McCarty Pottery, which draws thousands of shoppers a year, especially for their twice a year "cracked and imperfect" sale, when bargain hunters drive for hours, camp out in lawn chairs for days just to be first in line to purchase pieces that came out of the kiln not to McCarty's standards. The appeal of McCarty Pottery is such that people will fight over shards and happily pay for them.

Then there is the restaurant associated with it, known as The Gallery. Most shoppers and art lovers who make the pilgrimage to Merigold for the pottery usually stay and have lunch at The Gallery where they relax in the gracious bohemian atmosphere surrounded by original abstract art and fresh foliage and flowers arranged in McCarty vases. They feast on the chilled chicken salad plate or the hot shrimp crepes accompanied by a spinach casserole and Merigold tomatoes, a colorful concoction of stewed tomatoes and cornbread. Each diner receives small cornbread muffins and a small bowl of savory vegetable soup that prominently features okra and black-eyed peas. Other seasonal treats may also be brought to the table. Recently I was treated to a freshly picked large ripe fig accompanied by an

herbed cream cheese spread. Not-to-miss desserts include piping hot chocolate or caramel cobbler, with a generous scoop of vanilla ice cream. To enhance the experience, everything is served on McCarty pottery. Part of the mystique is that both the pottery studio and the restaurant post no signs showing where their businesses are. You "just have to know," which means that first time visitors must have good directions or ask someone when they get to town. I had been in Merigold several times before I had any idea of the location of the little studio where the pottery is sold. When I did venture behind those bamboo shrouded walls, I discovered not only beautiful works of art for sale, but a one-of-a-kind garden that visitors

are welcome to enjoy, filled with rustic sculptures, fountains, water-lily filled ponds, lush plants, moss covered rocks and vintage McCarty hanging vessels.

After living in the Delta awhile, I observed that one of the passions of its people is hunting. Created by centuries of annual flooding of the river before the levee system made living here possible, the loamy soil is considered too valuable for cultivation to be covered in forests. When the first settlers came to the area in the 1880s, they were lumbermen who came to cut the tightly grown virgin forests. Merigold itself is named for Frank Merigold who had a sawmill for making barrel staves, and the Merigold railroad spur was established there to transport his products. These forests had been filled with all kinds of prey for hunters, but by the 1920s, the forests were gone and so were the wild animals for hunting. Today throughout the miles and miles of table-flat land, almost every inch is in cultivation. So where do these lovers of the hunt go? I soon found out about the Merigold Hunting Club. It is one of the oldest hunting clubs in the state, chartered in 1921, as the once abundant game in the Mississippi Delta was rapidly becoming scarce due to loss of habitat and unrestricted hunting. Several men from Merigold organized a fish fry at the Big Blue Hole, a lake formed at the site of the levee break of 1912, the Beulah Crevasse, to discuss a way to band together to preserve the wildlife of the area and to help increase the herds. Merigold Hunting Club was born around that fishing hole and it became the early leader in wildlife conservation before

there were state game laws. They employed a game warden for many years before the state did. Together they leased valuable lands on both sides of the levee, which are still covered in forest. They restricted hunting of endangered game until the population was strengthened. They brought in deer from Mexico, Louisiana, and other places until they had some of the best deer anywhere. The soil near the Mississippi River produces nutritionally rich vegetation that allows the deer to grow larger here than in most other places. Today, Merigold Hunting Club still thrives as something right out of a Faulkner novel, and there are still many local families who maintain cabins there and participate in the club hunts.

After only a few days in the Delta, we discovered another Merigold treasure that reflects this love of hunting and good food, when we were treated to a wonderful meal at a restaurant in downtown Merigold known as Crawdad's. Crawdad's serves crawfish, when they are in season, spicy, steaming and piled high on covered trays. The restaurant is also known for its excellent cuisine, but it may be even better known for the menagerie of taxidermist-preserved wild game displayed on every wall in every room of the large rustic eatery. The owner, Andrew Westerfield, who is also the mayor of Merigold and an

attorney in nearby Cleveland, is an avid big game hunter. He and many of his friends from the Merigold and Cleveland areas frequently go to Africa, to Canada and the Northwest, and other places to pursue wild game. Many of their best specimens have been preserved and are displayed throughout the restaurant. Since the area between the levee and the Mississippi River is such a draw for hunters, many include a trip to Crawdads as a part of their hunting adventures.

I hadn't been in the Delta long before someone asked me if I had seen Po' Monkey's yet. Of course, I was intrigued by the name. It seems that Po' Monkey's is a well known juke joint located on a narrow road in Merigold in the middle of a cotton field on the Hiter plantation. Proprietor Willie Seaberry moved to the Hiter farm in 1954 at the age of thirteen, and later with his brother, began operating this juke joint in a former

sharecropper shack located on the farm as a place for field hands to gather after a long day's work, to let off a little steam, eat a pork chop sandwich or some barbeque, drink, dance, play pool, and hear some Blues. In 1963, Seaberry moved in to his juke joint. In my research, I learned that the house where Po' Monkey's is located was once the fre-

quent site in the 1940s for Sunday evening gatherings for the youth of Merigold hosted by the Methodist church's Epworth League. Teens from most of the Merigold churches would meet in town and walk out to the site, accompanied by Rev. Guinn, the Methodist pastor, where they would build a fire and roast hot dogs and marshmallows, sing, and "just have a good time." Today, Po' Monkey's is one of the most photographed locations in the Delta, having been featured in many national media outlets including *National Geographic* and the *New York Times*.

As I learned about all of these cultural traditions and places, I was intrigued that a town this small, located in the middle of thousands of acres of cotton, rice, and soybean fields, would be the center of such interesting cultural activity. Then I learned about another treasure only locals would probably know about. As I attended church in Merigold and got to know the families of the community, I became aware of the First Wednesday Potluck lunches at Merigold United Methodist Church. Now *that* is where one can find some of the real culinary artists of the Delta.

The regular potluck started back in the early 1970s with a quilting bee. Cack Meyer, a member of the Merigold United Methodist Church, worked for the Census Bureau during the 1970 Census. She was struck by the large number of older women in Merigold who were living alone. She found many who were lonely and depressed, hungry for conversation and human companionship. She encountered one neighbor who at two o'clock in the afternoon was in her nightgown and robe. The neighbor told her she was so lonely that all she felt like doing was crawling into bed and pulling the covers over herself. Meyer thought the community ought to do something about these lonely people all around them. She went back to the church and discussed the issue, and they decided that since most of the older women in Merigold knew how to sew, they should try to organize a quilting bee as a way to work together on a project while functioning as a social network of support for each other. They started meeting and eventually grew to be a large group, made up not only of Methodists, but Baptists and Presbyterians, too. They

had only one rule and that was "No malicious gossiping." At first they each brought a sandwich and then someone started bringing a dessert. They would begin their day with prayer and then get to work. They would stop and eat their lunches and then keep working throughout the afternoon. When cold weather came, Cack made a pot of soup to go with the sandwiches. Then another week another quilter said she would bring a casserole, and another said she would bring a cake—and the Merigold potluck lunch was born. Ladies who did not sew coordinated the kitchen activities. Eventually, the women began to invite their spouses and the men of the community who lived alone to join them for lunch.

After several years, the quilters began to be less able to sew and they finally quit meeting for quilting, but the potlucks have continued and grown to include dozens from the town of Merigold and nearby Shelby and Cleveland. A typical monthly lunch will include twenty-five to forty diners from all walks of life, and of all ages. And the food! Oh the food that those cooks concoct! It is always a gastronomic delight.

In the fall of 2004, when Delta State University's Capps Archives and Museum hosted the Smithsonian traveling exhibit, *Key Ingredients: America by Food*, which explored the rich culinary history of American food traditions, Capps Archives also led a project to capture the southern food traditions of the Mississippi Delta. From September 23 through November 13, 2004, the Capps Archives and Museum displayed the collected recipes, stories, photographs, and other memorabilia such as menus and tableware that represented Delta food traditions. As a part of this exhibit, they set up several special "food experiences," to showcase the best in Delta dining, including a very special lunch held at Merigold United Methodist Church on Wednesday, October 13, 2004. The members of the church outdid themselves and cooked many of their favorite dishes, proudly showcasing them and sharing with the guests on the Delta Bus Dinner Tour a bit of their tradition of meeting together for a large potluck meal that they had come to call the "groaning board" because the tables are so laden with food. Photos of this event were featured in *Delta Magazine*.

Following that event, I realized that this wonderful segment of culture—Merigold's food traditions and recipes—needed to be documented and I asked the members when they had last published a church cookbook. I was surprised to learn that their one and only cookbook had been published in the 1950s. After that discovery, I asked them if they would help me collect their favorite recipes and the stories related to them. I wanted to learn about the cooks, the families, and settings in which the recipes had been developed and used. In addition, I wanted to understand more about a small town that could foster such a unique cultural heritage of arts and juke joints and foods and gracious entertaining.

I talked to several members of the church and community about my desire to collect and preserve their recipes and food memories and received enthusiastic support. Each person I sat down with openly and lovingly shared warm memories of families gathered around the dining table, of dinners at the church, of Christmas feasts around tree lighting, and of large spaghetti dinner fundraisers by the Women's Society of Christian Service. Then I came upon a priceless treasure when Sue Rayner Latham told me she had the cookbook that the ladies of Merigold had handwritten as a wedding gift to her mother, Bess Field Rayner, in 1922. This handwritten cookbook had been kept and used throughout Mrs. Rayner's life. She had added many recipes through the years from friends and relatives, including special recipes from her own mother, Mollie Pemble Field, who was born in 1862. She had added some of her own favorite recipes through the years as well. I sat down with Mrs. Latham and her sister, Carolyn (Cack) Meyer, both lifelong active members of the Merigold community and of the United Methodist church there. They claim to everyone that they were "born on the front pew." On a warm spring afternoon, we sat down in Mrs. Latham's breakfast nook, in the home originally built by her parents, and the sisters went through the cookbook and told me what they knew of the people who had written the recipes in the collection and of the recipes they knew their mother used frequently throughout her life.

After that, I was given access to the handwritten notebook compiled by Virgie Park (Mrs. Leonard) Hiter, late matron of the Hiter Plantation in Merigold. These recipes also date to the 1920s and continue throughout her life as a homemaker. The crumbling notebook was discovered stored in the attic of her home when her grandson, Park Hiter moved into the family home place in 2007.

I was also able to secure a tattered copy of the 1950s cookbook compiled by the WSCS of Merigold Methodist Church, held together by a rubber band. In it were recipes from the next generation of Merigold's cooks, some of whom are still active today. Although it was published by the Methodist women, it features recipes from all over the community. It serves as a bridge between the 1920s recipes and the ones submitted by the cooks who laden today's "groaning board" with sumptuous cheese grits and layered salads and apple dumplings and dozens of other delicacies.

Author John T. Edge, director of the Southern Foodways Alliance, in his book *Southern Belly*, has given us a masterful collection of food traditions and treasures from all of the southern states, by featuring foods from tried and true restaurants across each of the states. In this book, he says that it would be ideal to be able to sit down at the tables of the local cooks in the homes of each region and get to know what they serve and the stories behind their food traditions, but without that kind of intimate access, he had to settle for going into public eating places and featuring them. His collection is a grand sweep of southern culinary traditions. By contrast, this collection serves as an up-close and personal look at one small town's food traditions in its homes, churches, and community events. Merigold, Mississippi is a unique place, but one with food traditions that may sound quite familiar, and may bring back a memory or two as you are reminded of your own, your mother's, or your grandmother's cooking.

Merigold's Cooks of the 1920s

1918 Statistical Report
Merigold-Alligator Charge
compiled by pastor
Rev. W. R. Lott

1 local preacher;
4 professions of faith;
24 additions by certificate and otherwise,
 21 removals by death and otherwise.
Present total membership, 203,
Adults baptized, 4,
Infants baptized, 8,
Number of churches in charge, 2,
Number of church buildings, 2;
Value, $3000.
Number of parsonages, 1,
Value, $3000,
Expended for churches and parsonage,
$1038
Insurance carried, $5750,
Premium paid, $73;
Number of Sunday schools, 2;

Estimate for the support of the preacher for
the year:
Merigold--$875.00
Alligator--$671.00, for a total $1546.00;
(Of this, amount, $220 is for the Presiding
Elder's salary)

Foun d in the 1918 quarterly report of Merigold Methodist Church:

"Nothing definite has been done for the poor among us as we are fortunate to have no one in dire need."

A Few Prominent Members of the Merigold Church
(Comments by pastor, 1918)

H. R. Park—One of the pioneers of church work around Merigold—For many years he was Sunday school superintendent and steward. The last office he still holds and is active.

Mrs. H. R. Park (Miss Lucy) is one of leading Sunday school teachers and has been very active in keeping the young people in the church.

Mrs. W. B. Parks is our faithful organist and also is teacher of intermediates. She is untiring in her efforts.

Bro. J. S. Fincher is Sunday school superintendent now. Though a young man, he is a workman that needeth not be ashamed. He is chairman of Board of Stewards. His wife is faithful S.S. teacher having a class of 20 or more small boys and girls.

Miss Ida Newby teaches the primaries in which position she is letting her light shine.

The following can be mentioned as faithful and active in some areas of the church: **F. E. Jones, H. B. Brooks, Dr. C. P. Thompson, H. M. Garland, R. C. Johnson, Mrs. R. C. Johnson, Mrs. W. H. Bernard, A. E. Nichols, Mrs. T. E. Perry, Mrs. W. M. Beck, W. M. Beck, Mrs. T. H. Lamastus.**

Merigold in 1922
The Historical Context

      Before we look at the recipes contributed by the Merigold cooks of 1922, it is interesting to consider their historical setting. Many people associate the Mississippi Delta with antebellum Old South, but only a narrow swath of land along the Mississippi River was developed and in cultivation by 1861. Merigold itself is a relatively new town, having been first settled in 1882 as a lumber town on a railroad spur named for Frank Merigold who came there with a sawmill. At that time, supplies and people had to come in on riverboats like the *Kate Adams*, to a landing on the Sunflower River. The virgin forests were filled with wild animals including panthers and bears. An early homemaker in Merigold Mrs. Frank Thomasson wrote of learning to use bear grease as a good shortening for biscuits because it never hardened. She also shared how she learned to prepare raccoon and bear meat in ways that were palatable. Will Dockery, who first came to Bolivar County from Hernando, Mississippi in 1888, said, "The country was covered with blue cane fifteen to twenty feet high and the land was rich as cream."

      In 1900 the Village of Merigold was chartered, claiming one hundred inhabitants. It was incorporated in 1908. Early pioneers of Merigold included A. M. Wynne, Walter B. Parks, J. M Goff, Henry R. Park, James R. Smith, Sr., Milton Jones, and Pat Dean. A dozen years later they were joined by industrious men like Leonard M. Hiter, Carl Jones, T. E. Pemble, and Edgar Rayner. About 1912 a water and sewer system was installed in Merigold and John B. Thomas built

several brick store buildings and a hotel. All of the buildings were quickly leased. Between 1910 and 1920, the population of Mississippi decreased, while that of Bolivar County increased by nearly 10,000 people. The Great War took many of its energetic young men away for its duration. They returned home anxious to build their careers, marry, and have families. The forests were gone and in their place were vast, open fields, cleared and productive beyond anyone's imagining. Northern investors like those who held the Birch Plantation across the river in Sunflower County, and men like candy mogul Vin Bremner, whose company produced the pink iced ginger cookie treat known as Stage Planks®, added to the flow of money into the area.

In 1919, Merigold proudly completed its new public school facility that featured 21 high school classrooms, and 9 elementary rooms plus a separate kindergarten building. The school had a gymnasium that would seat 500, a band room, and an agricultural/ vocational building. In 1924, the school had 420 pupils and 11 teachers. Walter Sillers of Rosedale claimed, "In 1924 Bolivar County led the world in the production of cotton—and long-staple cotton at that—producing from 85,000 to 125,000 bales annually."

The Great War was over and prosperity and optimism were the order of the day.

Of course, the men of a community of the time are most often listed in the documentary evidence, and it is often hard to even discern what a woman's given name was, since she was almost always referred to by the appellation of 'Mrs.' before her husband's name. But the lives of women were changing. As the Roaring Twenties began, for the first time in U.S. history, women could vote. They became more interested and involved in the world outside their homes. Women in the Twenties were more likely to work outside the home than ever before. By 1930, almost twelve percent of married women were employed outside the home. In Merigold, the wives of the planters and businessmen were typically college educated, extraordinary for women at that time, particularly in the South. This probably had much to do with the cultural atmosphere that persists there. Discussing the number of women in Merigold who were well educated, Mari Ana Pemble Davis said most of the women she had known there had gone to college. She said many of the Baptist girls were sent to Hillman College in Clinton. Many other girls went to Mississippi State College for Women in Columbus. Some, like she, went out of state to Stephens College in Missouri or Sarah Lawrence College, Randolph Macon College for Women, or in the case of Nell Wynne who returned to teach music at Delta State University in nearby Cleveland, to Northwestern in Chicago. Cack Rayner Meyer is a graduate of Louisiana State University while her sister Sue has a degree in English from Randolph-Macon College in Lynchburg, Virginia. Many women of Merigold came there as schoolteachers before marrying and becoming mothers, as was the case for Bess Field Rayner and Lexie Calhoun Pemble who came to Merigold to teach Latin. In an unusual twist, soon after her marriage, Bess Rayner became the teacher for the Big Brothers Bible Class, an ecumenical weekday study that consisted of about sixty of the businessmen and planters of Merigold.

Another benchmark of the 1920s was the increased availability of the automobile. Women embraced driving, although the roads in Bolivar County were still virtually impassible during rainy seasons outside of the towns. The first Bolivar County road was graveled in Rosedale in 1910, but it took several years to get to small towns like Merigold and the rural areas around them. J. T. Davis of Merigold told of one woman who accidentally left her hat at the restaurant of the three-story Midway Hotel in downtown Merigold, and had to wait several months for the roads to dry up to retrieve it. In 1922 the State Highway Department was formed and they began to improve the roads throughout the state including Bolivar County. The construction of U. S. Highway 61, which goes from Port Arthur, Canada to New Orleans, and includes Merigold, was authorized by the Highway Construction Act in 1936. Concrete paving of Highway 61 was completed from Mound Bayou to Cleveland by July 1938.

Life was not easy for Merigold residents in the Twenties. Besides the challenges of travel, they were always at the mercy of the weather for their crops and thus their livelihoods. In addition, many advances in medicine that we take for granted had not yet come. Penicillin was not discovered until 1928. In 1918 a major flu epidemic took its toll on Merigold. Pastor W. R. Lott of Merigold Methodist Church wrote in his quarterly conference report that Merigold church had lost sixteen members to the flu that year. They had to discontinue meetings of their youth group, the Epworth League, and even the meeting of the North Mississippi Annual Conference had to be postponed. Tuberculosis was a great threat, and at one time Dr. James Westerfield was afflicted with this disease and had to bring in another young doctor to cover his practice for several months while he recovered. This young man was Dr. J. P. McLaurin, Jr. who had grown up in Merigold, had just finished medical school, and was about to start his residency. Malaria was still a great threat in the Delta due to the ubiquity of the mosquito. A few years later, Merigold would be chosen as a site for testing procedures developed by the Rockefeller Foundation to stamp out the mosquito and the annual struggle with malaria, making Merigold one of the healthiest communities in the Delta.

Food historians see a change in the way people ate in the 1920s. Processed cereals became popular for breakfast and sandwiches emerged as an option for the midday meal, typically called "dinner" in the South as compared to "supper" for the evening meal. People became more health conscious and meals tended to become simpler. The new slimmer ideal for women as epitomized by the "flapper" called for lighter eating.

People in the 1920s had quite a sweet tooth, however, and most meals included cake or pie. More and cheaper foods were available to cooks at that time than ever before. Innovations in available foods in the 1920s included pancake mix, packaged desserts, and bouillon cubes. More and more food items were available canned on store shelves. The first commercially available peanut butter was introduced in 1922. Prior to that, nut butters had been made at home or in restaurants, were not sweetened, and the oils quickly separated. Peanut butter was often served at some of the most upscale parties of the time as a gourmet delicacy. With the introduction of Skippy® peanut butter, it became widely available, relatively inexpensive and was soon a staple for children's snacks. However, commercially sliced bread was not introduced until the late 1920s—so the convenient peanut butter and jelly sandwich as we know it today had to wait a little longer.

Food prices dropped 72 percent between 1920 and 1922. The international sugar market plummeted and in 1920, the price of sugar fell from 30 cents a pound in August to 8 cents a pound in December. Nationwide, Prohibition went into effect in January 1920 and continued until 1933, increasing the popularity of coffee, Coca-Cola, and ice cream sodas. However, this made little difference in Mississippi since there had been statewide laws against alcohol sales since 1908. In the Mississippi Delta, these laws had been largely overlooked, and alcohol use had continued. However, with a nationwide ban, alcohol became more difficult to acquire. Innovative cooks served fruit cocktail or shrimp cocktail as a first course.

In Merigold, Coca-Cola® was very popular. Drugstores in downtown Merigold had soda fountains, but also kept bottled Cokes cold and ready to go. For several years four of the young matrons of Merigold—Lexie Pemble, Bess Rayner, Emma Loys McLaurin, and Cora Lee Catchings—met every morning at ten o'clock in front of Clark Drugstore for their "Coke Break." They would pull up in their car, park, and Mr. Clark would immediately come outside bringing each a freshly opened, frosty bottle of Coke. They would sometimes have a pack of Nabs to go with their Cokes, but always they would sit in the car, drink their Cokes, and catch up on the events of the day. These women became known as the "Coke Crowd." Lexie Pemble's daughter Mari Ana says, "You'd think they held stock in Coca-Cola the way they drank it. It was served at just about every event."

These women had the luxury of getting to take their morning Coke break because all but one of them had a cook at home preparing lunch. These cooks, I am told, worked under the supervision of the matrons who selected and planned the meals and instructed their help in how each dish was to be prepared.

Coffee was also very important in most homes in Merigold. Even today at the monthly Merigold potluck, one of the first things I noticed was that no iced tea—the requisite beverage of just about every Southern gathering—was served, only coffee and ice water. Mari Ana Pemble Davis believes this tradition is a result of many of the early transplants to Merigold being from Centreville, very close to Louisiana where coffee is very important. She says,"Tea just never did catch on in Merigold." Every Sunday morning today, Merigold United Methodist Church has coffee hour immediately following morning services and the coffee is made by Cack Meyer who learned to make coffee while she was a student at LSU—"strong and black." They have added hot cocoa to the coffee hour, though.

Merigold in 1922 did not yet have electricity in its homes. That was to come in about four years. Refrigeration was accomplished by keeping food in an icebox. There was an icehouse in downtown Merigold by the railroad track, next door and at a right angle to present day Crawdad's Restaurant. The building is still there. According to the recollections of Sue Latham and Mari Ana Pemble Davis, Mr. Blaylock ran the icehouse. A housewife would place a card in the window indicating how much ice she wanted, and Mr. Blaylock would come by and place the requested size block of ice into the ice compartment of the icebox, often kept on the back porch. Latham said Mr. Blaylock made his rounds in a little "spinning jenny" pickup. Cooking was done in most households of the time on a gas stove, although some cooks still used wood stoves. Water would often be heated in a reservoir attached to these stoves. When Merigold homes received electricity near the end of the decade, it made possible electric lights and refrigeration. As Sue Rayner Latham remembered getting their first electric refrigerator, "I can't remember the year, but I remember it. We thought we were sittin' in town, sure enough."

Mr. Charlie Clark was the enterprising owner of the drug store on the corner in the first brick building in Merigold. This historic building has in recent history hosted the semi-annual art show and sale known as Merigold Marketplace. Mr. Clark's well-known slogan was "If we don't have it, you don't need it, but if you want it, we can have

it by Thursday." He served sandwiches and operated a soda fountain in the drug store. In later years he moved to a building across the street and also sold furniture and appliances. Some say he was such a good salesman he had sold every household in town a refrigerator and washing machine a year or two before the town received electricity by encouraging everyone to beat the rush that would surely come when everyone's homes were wired. That may be an exaggeration, but he certainly was a memorable character in the community. Sue

Latham remembers accompanying her friend Voncile Brown when Brown's mother was dating Mr. Clark after Voncile's father's death. "I will never forget the first time I went to a picture show on a Sunday. I went with them and they wanted to go to a picture show in Shaw. I thought 'The devil's gonna get me right there in Shaw.' I was scared to death. You just didn't go to the picture show on a Sunday.' Sue adds that Mr. Clark "was a jolly man and he had little fat red-apple cheeks and he died with hiccups, of all things. Died of hiccups."

In the 1920s new innovations such as toasters and vacuum cleaners began to be available to make housekeeping easier. Surveys showed that by the mid-1920s, the time spent by women in meal preparation and cleanup had fallen from 44 hours per week to under 30 hours. Almost all of the matrons of Merigold whose husbands were business-men or planters had cooks and gardeners to help them. Children typically grew up help-ing tend the family garden and preserve its produce. In an interview with the daughters of Ed and Bess Rayner, Sue Latham and Cack Meyer emphasized the importance to the families of Merigold of having a garden. Cack said, "Mother had a huge garden."

Sue said, " She had a cook and she had a yardman and a man who came to milk. And we had to wash the buckets for her. Cack and I didn't just sit around and read fun-ny books. We didn't have television, of course, but she made us work."

Cack said, "Mother worked in the garden right along with [the yardman]. She raised okra, butterbeans, potatoes—we had so many potatoes one year we peeled and canned little potatoes."

Sue added, "She raised some corn, not much; lettuce and radishes, and green onions."

Cack added, "And eggplant. She had her own little planter box—seedbed—with a little window on it right outside the house, so that when it came time to plant, she had all these plants al-ready raised. She didn't have to buy anything ex-cept the seeds. And she would share those plants with anybody that wanted them; they would be so thick, see, in that seedbed. It had a glass—it had an old window on the top of that seedbed, right there outside her bedroom window where she could keep an eye on it. It was about the size of a table. It was an old wooden box down in the ground with this window over it. When it would be really, really warm, she would go out there and raise that window up so they could get plenty of sunshine. When it was real cold, it was warm inside it from the sun. "

Sue continued, "Everybody had a garden."

Cack said, "Some people worked them alone. Other people had some help, usually off the farm. We canned everything that wouldn't move! We canned vegetable soup with all the okra and tomatoes and there was an onion that she had. We would put up what she called 'soup mix.' We had some peach trees and some pears and fig trees, so when it came time, we had jelly and preserves."

Almost every meal in the typical Merigold home of that time featured vegetables and fruits served fresh from the garden or preserved through the laborious process of canning or drying. Most recipe books collected by housewives of the time did not feature recipes for cooking vegetables. These techniques were so basic to everyday life that they were just learned throughout a girl's growing up as she watched and assisted her mother in preparing them. More typical are recipes for making pickles or relishes, which allowed a cook to show off her creativity. I asked Cack and Sue about their mother's cooking of garden vegetables. I said, "One thing I have noticed is that there were no vegetable dishes written down and I have assumed it was because everyone just cooked what came from the garden."

Cack said, "That's right."

"Well, tell me how your mother prepared her butterbeans, for instance."

Cack replied, "I'll tell you how she'd cook them. Of course, if we had canned—later frozen—butterbeans, she'd drop them in boiling water. Then Mother would always have her seasoning in another container. She would melt her butter and add sugar and salt and pepper—"

Sue added, "She'd have bacon grease, too."

Cack agreed, "Well, most of the time. And when she would wait until they were just almost tender and then she would add her seasonings. She would never start out cooking them with it in there. I do that same thing today when I cook my English peas and butterbeans."

"How did she cook her green beans?"

Cack said, "We cooked green beans with fat meat."

Sue added, "And they cooked a LONG time—slow cooked with salt meat—fat back. We raised pigs for a while, but then Daddy had a commissary and he had salt meat in there."

You will notice when you read the recipes that many are very short on cooking directions. It was just assumed that a woman would know what to do with the list of ingredients to turn them into a pie or cake or a jar of pickles. Later, when Bess added her own choices of recipes, she often wrote down only the barest of details so that she could cook the dish, not writing out those steps she would know how to do from experience. This makes the collection a little hard to follow, but it is still an interesting glimpse into what homemakers of the 1920s wanted to cook and serve their families and friends.

The average American family in the 1920s liked for every meal to include sweets, they sometimes experimented with new and different dishes, and usually served meals at regular times each day. Very popular were congealed dishes and fancy desserts. Many of these recipes call for "gelatine" which was the way Charles Knox spelled his granulated gelling agent, introduced in 1890, which greatly simplified the use of gelatin in the home.

The first Jell-O® product was introduced in 1897, before electric refrigeration. Cooks had to trust the icebox or set the mixture outside on a cold day to congeal. Although oleomargarine had been invented, cooks in Merigold still relied on butter in the 1920s, since almost everyone had a cow for milk. Dairy states fought the marketing of oleomargarine tooth and nail and succeeded in having laws passed forbidding it to be sold with yellow coloring in it. It was naturally white and was more like vegetable shortening. Without the yellow color to look like butter, the dairy lobby believed it would not be as appetizing. Notice that a common way for cooks to measure butter for recipes was to call for butter "the size of an egg." Foods popular in 1920s kitchens were fruit cocktail, tea sandwiches, fancy salads, pineapple upside down cake cooked in an iron skillet, and chafing dish recipes.

The homemakers and cooks of Merigold were living in exciting times. There was a boom in cotton prices in the late twenties, until the catastrophic crash of 1929. There were several difficult years for everyone during the Great Depression, but in the 1930s, Merigold had 36 stores and a three-story hotel. Its population was eight hundred in the thirties, and that usually doubled on Saturdays when the people who lived on the surrounding farms would come in to town. There were even some restaurants and "lunch counters" there. Mari Ana Pemble Davis recalled Mr. Luther's restaurant in the 1920's, which was located facing the railroad track next door to Rayner's Hardware, in the row where Crawdad's is today. It was in the building where the Slodov's store later operated. Davis recalls that Mr. Luther loved track and he would give winners of track events at Merigold High School a piece of his famous lemon pie if they would come by. She ran track and she loved his lemon pie. He also served hamburgers and plate lunches. Bess Rayner had his recipe for waffles in her cookbook, but the page it was written on was so damaged, the recipe could not be deciphered.

Merigold in the 1920s was often a bustling place, and by most accounts a great place to live. The homemakers there took pride in making sure their families were well clothed, well educated, well mannered, and well fed.

Heirloom Measurements
Teacup=scant ¾ cup
Butter the size of an egg=2 ounces or ¼ cup
Pinch or Dash= the amount you can pick up between thumb and first two fingers; less than 1/8 teaspoon
1 peck=2 gallons dry

Temperatures
Slow oven= 300°
Moderate oven=350°
Quick oven=375°-400°
Hot oven= 400°-425°
Very Hot Oven=450°-475°

The 1922 Rayner Cookbook

In 1922, young Merigold schoolteacher, Miss Bess Field, of Centreville, Mississippi, married Edgar Dewitt Rayner, who had come to the Mississippi Delta in 1911. Rayner had come first to Silver City to work for a cousin with a drug store, before moving to the promising new town of Merigold. Rayner had grown up in Bowling Green, Mississippi, a small community near Durant. Rayner's career as business owner and planter had to be delayed while he served in the U. S. Army during World War I, eventually becoming a machine gunner instructor. At the end of his service, he was a sergeant. Bess Field had come to Merigold to teach following her education at Mississippi State College for Women at Columbus, at the suggestion of her brother, Dr. C. L. Field who had come from Centreville to practice medicine in nearby Shaw. She also had a cousin, T. E. Pemble who had arrived in Merigold from Centreville to work in 1910. Edgar and Bess were married on July 19, 1922.

At a wedding shower held on August 11, 1922 for Bess and Edgar Rayner, women of the Merigold community passed around a blank bound cookbook and each contributed a favorite recipe to the various sections, handwritten on the pages in flowing fountain pen ink. The title on the hardback cover reads *Recipes: My Friends and My Own*. The book has thumb-divided sections as follows: Breads, Beverages, Soups, Fish, Eggs, Entrees, Meats, Vegetables, Salads, Puddings and Pastry, Custards, Jellies, and Ices, Cakes, The Chafing Dish, and Miscellaneous.

Bess and Edgar Rayner were married for fifty-three years. They had two daughters, Carolyn, known as "Cack," who married John Meyer, and Sue, who married Billy Latham, also of Merigold. The Rayners were very active in Merigold Methodist Church.

Bess Rayner became known as a gracious hostess, a devoted gardener, and wonderful cook. She was the one who most frequently hosted the showers or luncheons for the brides and graduates in Merigold. Her daughters remember that she usually served chicken salad sandwiches with the crusts trimmed—and no mayonnaise—and various cakes, often *petit fours* purchased in nearby Cleveland from Willard Samuels' bakery. She always decorated with fresh flowers from her yard when they were in season—especially from her collection of more than three hundred rose bushes.

Mary Aileen Lee Colucci recalled this experience with Mrs. Rayner's entertaining: "When Mary Hull and I graduated from high school, Mrs. Rayner and Sue hosted a luncheon for us. I do not recall how many people were invited, but it was not a small group. The entire event was nothing short of elegant with marvelous food, beautifully displayed and served, and perfect in every way. I have attended other luncheons and dinner parties, but there is no doubt that theirs was by far the best."

Another testament to her memorable entertaining was when longtime Merigold physician and his wife, James A. and Shirley Westerfield, celebrated their silver wedding anniversary, they dressed up in their wedding finery—her wedding dress and his military dress uniform, for he was serving in the Aleutian Islands during World War II at the time of their marriage—and paid an anniversary visit to the Rayners in commemoration of her having given them their wedding shower.

 Edgar Rayner eventually acquired a large plantation and was president of the Smith and Wiggins cotton gin. He owned the Rayner Hardware, which also functioned as the commissary of his farming operation, and sold caskets before there was an undertaker available in the area. It was located on the lot facing the railroad tracks, now occupied by Crawdad's Restaurant. He was county supervisor from 1932-1936 and then ran for sheriff against Joe Smith. He lost the election by one vote, but was elected overwhelmingly four years later. E. D. Rayner was sheriff during WWII. He died in 1975.

At Bess Rayner's death in 1985, the cookbook was passed on to her daughter, Sue Rayner Latham, who has kept it as a treasured heirloom since. For the purposes of this collection and for our examination of the food heritage of Merigold and the surrounding Mississippi Delta, it is an invaluable primary document of the special dishes prepared by its cooks of almost a century ago.

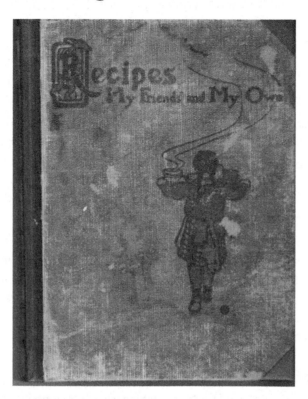

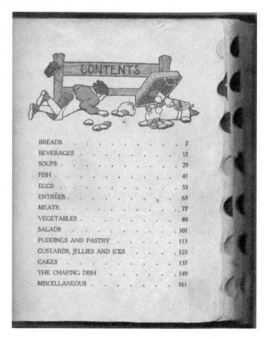

CONTENTS

On the first inside page of the handwritten gift from the women of Merigold is written, "Mr. and Mrs. Edgar Rayner, August 11, 1922—

The way to a man's heart is through his stomach."

This page is signed, "Mrs. Jiggs," who was Velma Smith, the wife of Albert Smith, the brother and sometime business associate of prominent Merigold businessman J. R. "Big Daddy" Smith, Sr. who was one of Merigold's early developers, coming to town in 1890 as the Depot agent and then buying land (ultimately operating 30,000 acres in row crops) and establishing businesses including a cotton gin.

Sue Rayner Latham said, "The reason for the name for Albert as 'Mr. Jiggs' was that he was a small man that wore a hat just on top of his head and he looked just like Jiggs from the comic strip 'Maggie and Jiggs.'" Velma was called "Mrs. Jiggs." She was small, "a pretty lady who wore her hair in a bun" and a member of the Baptist church, recalls Mari Ana Pemble Davis. The Albert Smiths lived in a lovely white clapboard house directly facing Merigold Methodist Church and next door to the park. It appears that Mrs. Smith was the organizer of the cookbook project for the Rayner shower. *From the opening page of the 1922 Cookbook, handwritten by "Mrs Jiggs":*

Recipe for a Day

Take a dash of water cold
And a little leaven of prayer
A little bit of sunshine gold
Dissolved in the morning air,
Add to your meal some merriment
And a thought for kith and kin,
And then as a prime ingredient,
A plenty of work thrown in,
But spice it all with the essence of love
And a little whiff of play;
Let a wise old Book and a glance above
Complete the well-spent day.

Following are the recipes and some things I have learned about their authors:

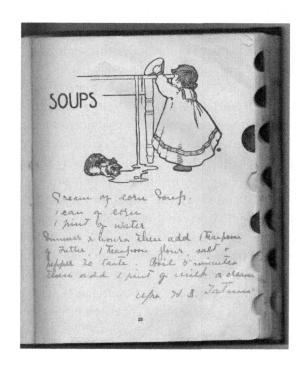

Cream of Corn Soup

1 can of corn
1 pint of water

Simmer 2 hours, then add **1 teaspoon of butter, 1 teaspoon flour; salt, and pepper to taste.** Boil 5 minutes and then add **1 pint of milk or cream.**

Mrs. H. R. Tatum

Lobster Creamed

1 can lobster
1 small onion
2 teaspoons celery seeds
2 cups of rich milk or canned milk
1 teaspoon of butter

Cut onion fine and put in skillet with enough water to cover, and boil until done. Add salt, pepper, celery seeds, and butter. Add milk. Mix a little flour with milk and stir in. Add lobster and stir until slightly thickened. Serve on toast. Can be used as an entrée or entire chafing dish supper.

Mrs. Frank Wynne

Mrs. Frank Wynne was Edna Grove Wynne. She had once been an actress in the theater, although locals do not agree on where. Some say Broadway, some California. Mari Ana Pemble recalled that Edna and Frank met in Merigold and that she may have come there to teach school.

Sue Latham remembered, "She would dress herself up every morning and walk to town. And we were all kind of scared of her. We didn't understand anybody who was dressed like she was because she didn't have on just a cotton housedress. She put on her finery. And that is who put this recipe in here for Creamed Lobster. Now, it says you use a can of lobster. I didn't even know you could buy canned lobster back then, but I guess you could."

Cack Meyer added, "She had grace—unbelievable grace—when she walked. She never left her house that she didn't have on gloves and a hat and the best that she had. In her later years when she was not well, she was never still; she constantly walked and never went without all of that."

She had two children, Frank and Ted. Frank Wynne, Jr. spent thirty months as a prisoner of war in Japan and his children were Frank III, Diane, and Pat. The Wynne's daughter was also named Edna Grove Wynne, but she was always known as "Ted." Ted married Mari Ana Davis's mother Lexie Pemble's only brother, Orville Calhoun, and he first worked as a bookkeeper on the Birch Plantation in Merigold, but he then went to Bowling Green to business school and later moved to Florida to manage the office of a large cigar company there.

Meat Loaf

1 lb. pork
1 lb. beef
1 large onion
6 crackers
3 eggs
Melted butter
1 can of tomatoes

Grind meat, onion, and crackers in food chopper. Season well with salt and pepper, then mix in the three well-beaten eggs and melted butter. Form a loaf, put in well-greased pan, cover with whole can of tomatoes. Bake in moderate oven until golden brown. This slices better when cold.

Mrs. Aldron E. Davis

Sue Latham said, "That's Mrs. Sarah Davis and she taught the children's Sunday school class for years and when we bought a piano—when we needed one for that class so bad, it had a memorial plaque to Mrs. Sarah Davis."

Cack added, "It is down stairs now. That's the piano we have in the fellowship hall. She was real petite, but she taught children for years and their home is right directly across the street from the Baptist church."

Sue continued, "The house next door to her is where [my husband] Billy lived, where Mrs. Latham lived. It had belonged to Mr. Aldron Davis' father, Mr. Jeff Davis, and he was killed—the train hit him one day at noon here on the railroad track in front of where Crawdad's is now. He had a drugstore, too, on the corner, which is now the Gong Company. That was the Davis Drug Store. Mrs. Sarah Davis was killed, too, in a car wreck. She had a son named Aldron, Jr,. and they had a daughter named Elizabeth who was badly afflicted and Mrs. Davis cared for her. Everyone wondered what she would do when Mrs. Davis was killed."

Chicken Pie

Cut and joint **one young chicken**, cover with **cold water** and let boil gently until tender. Season with **salt and pepper**, and thicken gravy with **two tablespoonfuls of flour** mixed smooth with **a cup of sweet milk**; add **two hard boiled eggs** chopped fine, also a piece of **butter** the size of an egg. Pour into baking dish lined with **rich crust**. Cover with strips of crust and bake until brown.

Mrs. Charles. Gramling

Violet Gramling's husband was the manager of the Smith and Wiggins farm known as Plenty Hell Farm, now part of the Rogers Hall Plantation. They lived east of town near where Rushing Winery was in the 1970s. She taught children in the Sunday school at the Methodist church.

Chicken Salad

Cut **cold boiled chicken** fine. Add half as much **celery,** cut fine. Season with **salt and pepper**. Mix with **French dressing**. Just before serving, stir in some **Mayonnaise**. Arrange on **lettuce leaves** and cover with thick Mayonnaise. Chopped **walnut or pecan** meats may be used, if preferred.

Mrs. J. E. Taylor

Mrs. J. E. Taylor lived west of Merigold next to where Beth and Lex Davis live today on the Pemble Plantation.

Stuffed Tomato Salad

"To Serve at Afternoon Tea"

Cheese Crackers

Ice tea or lemonade

Scoop out **tomatoes** and chop with **peppers, olives, pimentos, celery seed** and mix with **salad dressing**, the kind more preferable. Stuff tomatoes, put a small spoonful of salad dressing on top, and sprinkle with paprika. Serve on lettuce or cabbage leaf.

"Pussy Cat"

Red and White Salad

1 small head of cabbage

3 large tomatoes

2 large bell peppers

Sauce:

½ bottle of tomato catsup

¼ teaspoon salt

1 level teaspoon sugar

Juice of 1 lemon

2 tablespoons sweet cream,

       or a bit of chopped ham or grated cheese

Chop the cabbage very fine. Place in ice water for 30 minutes to crisp. Then add chopped tomatoes and peppers and dressing and place on ice until ready to serve. Serve on a lettuce leaf when possible to obtain it.

Mrs. W. B. (Mamie) Parks

Mamie Wynne Parks was the daughter of early Merigold developer A. M. Wynne. She was the sister of the early physician in Merigold Dr. A. M Wynne, and aunt of Shirley Wynne Westerfield and Nell Wynne. When Mamie was growing up, the Wynnes spent summers in Merigold and then lived in Memphis to attend school in the fall because there were no schools available in Merigold at that time. Mamie and her sisters attended St. Agnes and her brothers attended Christian Brothers. Her father owned a general store, hardware, and saloon in Merigold and represented the Klein Stave Company. He brought in young Walter B. Parks to manage the store; W. B. and Mamie were married in 1900 and Parks bought Pat Dean's store, and then bought his father-in-law's store. Mr. Wynne then returned to live in Memphis.

Mamie Parks traveled extensively, was a leader in the Methodist church, and a philanthropist. She was very involved in the building of the new Methodist church facility that was completed in 1920. One of the largest stained glass windows was placed there by her. The Parks built an impressive three-story home with rock veneer facing the park. Nell Wynne remembered that it included what Mamie referred to as the "Cure Room," which was a screened porch lined with beds for summer sleeping. This was in the days just after Kellogg's Corn Flakes were introduced and there was a new health consciousness in the way people lived and ate. Cack and Sue said, "They had a big house and servants' quarters out over the garage and the barn where the hostler and the maid stayed. It was separate and it was just off Orchard Drive. Anyway, everybody was just in awe of her." Mari Ana Pemble Davis said that the third floor of the house was a ballroom. The house burned after the deaths of Mr. and Mrs. Parks. Mrs. Parks wrote a brief history of Merigold before her passing. An excerpt shows her love of language and of her hometown:

"I would that I could wave a wand and produce upon a silver screen the pictured topography of the part of the earth's surface upon which Merigold was builded.

"For the benefit of those who did not hear the history of Bolivar County I will recapitulate a portion of that history, just enough to give you a picture of the jungle which man's prowess changed into one of the most progressive and live wire parts of the delta.

"Great forest trees and an undergrowth of evergreen cane covered the flat surface of the country. Great clinging vines of grape and muscadine clinging to tops of trees festooned the forests through which wildcats, panthers, wolves, bear, deer and other wild things roamed. Millions of beautiful birds nested in the giant trees, making the forest brilliant in color, awakening the glad morning hours with sweetest love notes from myriads of little feathered songsters, echoing and re-echoing praises in jubilant songs to the Creator of the universe.

"Other than the voices of nature breaking the silence of the virgin forests were the ringing axes and lusty songs of the sturdy crew clearing the right of way and laying rails for the mighty iron horse that was soon to go thundering through the great Mississippi Valley."

Tomato Salad

Blanch and slash **tomatoes** in fourths; fill with thinly sliced **cucumbers, asparagus,** and chopped **stuffed olives** served with **Thousand Island dressing on lettuce**.

Meida B. Gilbert

Marshmallow Pudding

Mix together the following:
1 tablespoonful of Knox®gelatine,
    dissolved in a little water
1 cup boiling water
Pour over 4 egg whites, beaten stiff
Add **1 cup of sugar**. Beat all together until it begins to stiffen.
Divide. Color 1 part pink to which add **one cup chopped nuts**
and add **one cup of crushed pineapple** to the white part. Congeal.
To serve, slice and serve with **whipped cream** [*The Rayner daughters remembered their mother serving this dish every Christmas colored red and green.*]

Mrs. John. S. Fincher

Gertie Fincher was the mother of Ethlyn Speakes and grandmother of Larry Speakes, the journalist from Merigold who became press secretary to President Ronald Reagan. Bess and E. D. Rayner lived with the Finchers during the first months of their marriage. Mr. John Fincher was the bookkeeper for E. D. Rayner's businesses and served as Sunday School Superintendent at Merigold Methodist Church for many years. According to Sue Latham, "Mrs. Fincher was the pillar of the church. She was just a wonderful woman. She taught us all in Sunday school. She just was one of the best women I knew. I remember when I had a birthday and I was about six, and mother's sister-in-law who had recipes in this book—here's one right here—Lizbeth Field, who was Uncle Sam's wife, died and was buried on my birthday. Mother, of course, was gone to Centreville to take care of Uncle Sam. And I thought, 'I'm not going to have anything for my birthday.' I was sort of spoiled. And Mrs. Fincher brought over a birthday cake with little yellow flowers all around it. I'll never forget it. I did have a birthday cake even with my mother gone." Sue said that was in about 1935.

Cack Meyer added, " Mrs. Fincher took in boarders. She was a wonderful cook. She didn't have people who lived there, but she had a boarding table. She had a big square table right next to her kitchen and you just were hoping you could eat there because her food was just wonderful." When I asked her what Mrs. Fincher was best known for, I was expecting to hear about a certain dish, but Cack responded immediately, "Her gentleness. She was a large lady, but she was so kind." Mrs. Fincher, along with her sister Mamie Kealhofer, had a boarding table serving twenty to thirty people. People in the community would call ahead and reserve a place at her table. Diners ate around her dining table or on her enclosed side porch. She also had the assistance of Day, her longtime cook. Mari Ana Pemble Davis said, "Oh, you considered yourself very lucky if you were able to go to Mrs. Fincher's for Sunday dinner. It was all just delicious. Everything she cooked was just wonderful."

Lemon Pie

¾ cup of sugar
¾ cup of boiling water
1 tablespoon of flour
1 grated lemon
1 teaspoon of butter
Yolks of 2 eggs

Mix sugar, flour and boiling water and cook two minutes. Then add butter, yolk, and lemon. Cook for five minutes and put in baked crust and cool. Reserve whites of eggs, beaten lightly with two tablespoonfuls of sugar. Spread meringue over pie and brown.

Mrs. J. E. Kinsey

Mrs. Kinsey was the wife of the Baptist pastor in Merigold at the time.

Raisin Pie

For two pies—
Yolks of 4 eggs
2 cup fulls sweet milk
1 ½ cup sugar
2 tablespoons vinegar
Grate "a little" nutmeg
3 tablespoons butter
1 package raisins
Beat whites lightly—spread on top.

Mrs. E. M. Causey

As you can see, the ladies were not long on directions, because all young brides were expected to know the basics of cooking.

Golden Custard

Divide yolk and white of **six eggs**. Beat with yolk **six tablespoons sugar, one teaspoon sifted flour, 1 teaspoon melted butte**r. Have on stove **one quart boiling milk**. Pour over this paste and return to stove and stir till thickens to consistency of starch. Remove from stove and drop the whites on top after having added **six table-spoons sugar** and beating stiff. Set in hot stove a moment to brown over. Serve cold.

Mrs. R. C. Johnston

Mrs. Johnston was the mother of Annie Celeste Bernard. She was a tall woman who reminded Mari Ana Davis of Popeye's Olyve Oil. Sometimes she would go to her neighbor, Mrs. Steve Johnston's (no relation) and say, "I'm having a sinking spell. I need a piece of your cornbread."

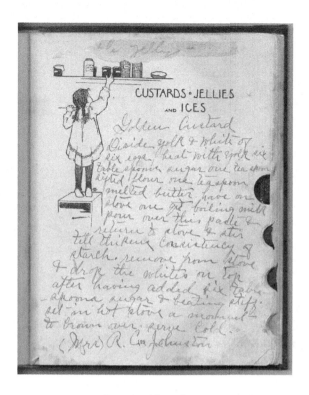

Fruit Sherbet

4 cups of sugar

4 cups of water

4 egg whites, beaten

4 lemons

4 oranges

4 bananas

Set the sugar and water on the side of stove and let it simmer but not boil until it melts and forms a syrup. Set off and cool. When ready to freeze, cut up bananas and oranges and squeeze the lemon juice all into the syrup; put in [crank ice cream] freezer and freeze until almost stiff. Open and add the stiff whites of eggs and turn until very stiff and serve. A small can of grated pineapple adds to this; also other fruits may be substituted, but always use the lemons with any combination.

This will make one gallon when frozen. The eggs make it puff up at the very last. One person may eat four saucers of this without injury to the digestive organs, unless they are newly married, in which case only two saucers should be eaten. In case a pain does seize you after eating, an excellent remedy will be one tablespoon of Sloan's liniment and ½ cup of castor oil.

Mrs. Guy Waldrop

Mrs. Guy (Etta) Waldrop was the sister of Carl Jones and a member of the Baptist church in Merigold. She volunteered with the Sunbeams and GA's there. She owned and operated the only beauty shop in Merigold, had beautiful white hair, and was known for her expertise in arranging hair in "finger waves."

Checkerboard Cake

Light Part
2 cups pastry flour
2 level teaspoons full of baking powder
1 ½ cups granulated sugar
½ cup butter
½ cup water
1 teaspoon vanilla
Whites of four eggs

Cream butter and sugar. Add water and dry ingredients alternately, then whites of eggs, and beat hard.

Dark Part

2 cups pastry flour
2 level teaspoons full of baking powder
1 cup brown sugar
½ cup butter
½ cup water
½ teaspoon each of cloves, cinnamon, and nutmeg
Yolks of 4 eggs
1 oz. melted chocolate

Sift flour once, then measure; add baking powder, and sift three times. Cream butter and sugar; add yolks and beat hard, then add flour and water alternately.

Put in square layer pans in stripes, light and dark alternately, and place together dark to light.

Icing

1 ½ cups confectioner's sugar with just enough **cream** to spread. Flavor with **vanilla**.

Eunice Taylor

Date Loaf Cake

1 # [lb.] dates
1 cup flour
½ teaspoon salt
4 eggs
1 # [lb.] English walnut meats
2 teaspoons baking powder
1 cup sugar
1 teaspoon vanilla

Have dates and nuts as whole as possible. Sift over them flour, baking powder, salt which have been sifted together first, then add sugar. Sift again. Beat in yolks and fold in whites. Bake one hour in moderate oven. "<u>Delicious.</u>"

Mrs. E. C. (Cam) Harrington
August 9, 1922

Angel Food Cake

Whites of 8 eggs
½ teaspoon of Cream of Tartar
½ teaspoon of flavoring
1 cup of sugar
1 cup of flour

Beat whites of eggs a little, then add cream of tartar. Beat again. Add flavoring. Add sugar. Beat lots. Then fold in one cup of flour, which has been sifted several times. Bake in slow oven.

Mrs. Steve (Mamie) Johnston

Home Fruit Cake

3 teacups flour, sifted 3 times with 3 teaspoons baking powder
1 teacup brown sugar
1 teacup molasses
½ teacup butter
3 eggs
1 teaspoon each cloves, spice, nutmeg and cinnamon
½ # [lb.] each raisins, currants, figs, and citron cut fine
1 teacup nut meats

Mix fruit and spices well with one cup flour day before making cake. Bake in slow oven 2 ½ or 3 hours.

Mrs. T. E. Perry

Chocolate Layer Cake

1 cup butter
2 cups sugar
3 cups flour
6 eggs

Mix and bake in layers. Put together with filling made as you do fudge.

Unsigned

White Cake

2 cups sugar
3 cups flour
8 egg whites
1 cup sweet milk
1 teaspoon vanilla
3 teaspoons baking powder
1 cup butter

Cream butter and sugar. Add sweet milk and flour that has been mixed with baking powder and last, fold in egg whites that have been beaten very stiff.

Mrs. W. H. Bernard

Mrs. W. H. Bernard was the former Annie Celeste Johnston. She was a student at MSCW at the same time Bess Field attended. She was known as a good cake baker. She loved music and played piano at Merigold Methodist Church on Sunday nights.

Fruit Bavarian Cream

Soak one-fourth box of **gelatine** in one-fourth cup of cold **water**; cook **two egg yolks**, beaten with **one-fourth cup of sugar** and a **dash of salt**, in **one cup of hot milk**, till smooth like soft custard, and strain into a pan set in ice water. When cool, add **one-half cup of fresh fruit juices** (cherries, raspberries, strawberries, oranges, or half currants and half banana, mashed, sifted, and sweetened to taste.) When it begins to thicken, fold in **one cup of thick cream whipped stiff**, and turn into small moulds; then turn out and serve with some of the fresh fruit for a garnish, or the syrup for a sauce.

Cora Baker Lee

Cora Baker Lee was the daughter of Mrs. and Mrs. J. B. Lee. She later married Lee Catchings and lived in a big brick house. She had no children.

Spanish Pickles

1 gallon cucumbers
12 gallons cabbage
1 quart onions
½ dozen green peppers

Grind through food chopper and measure after grinding. Salt and let stand 12 hours, then drain. Take **3 quarts vinegar, 1 ounce black pepper, 1 ounce ginger, 1 ounce celery seed, 2 ounces white mustard seed, 1 ounce horseradish, grated, 1 quart sugar, 1 ounce turmeric, and 1 tablespoonful alum**. Put all together in a pan and let come to a boil. Put in jars and seal.

Mrs. W. H. Graves

Mrs. W. H. (Ruth) Graves was the wife of the Merigold depot agent. They had two daughters and a son.

Cheese Fondant

Heat **one pint of sweet milk** in a double boiler. Put into it **one cup of finely cut cheese, one teacup of** cracker crumbs. When cheese is melted, put in 3 well-beaten eggs and 1 tablespoon of butter. Add **dash of red pepper**. When it begins to thicken, turn into baking dish, put into stove and bake, light brown.

Ida M. Baker

Ida M. Baker was a sister of J. B. Lee and the aunt of Cora Baker Lee Catchings of Merigold.

This concludes the recipes that appear to have been written down on the day of the shower. It appears that Bess Rayner added the recipes that follow quite soon after the shower in the early days of her marriage.

As any bride would do, Bess collected some of her favorite recipes from her own mother, **Mrs. Samuel Caleb (Mary "Mollie" Pemble) Field.** She was originally from Centreville, Mississippi, born during the Civil War in 1862. She died in the 1950s. The following are from Bess' mother:

Cheese Omelet

1 cup scalded milk
1 cup soft stale bread,
    diced fine
1 cup mild cream cheese, in small pieces
1 tablespoon butter
 3 eggs
Salt to taste

Add bread to scalded milk and cook till smooth. Then add cheese, butter, salt, and egg yolks, slightly beaten. Beat egg whites stiff and fold in. Bake in medium oven 20 minutes.

Cheese Cake Pie

To yolk of every **egg**, add tablespoon **sugar** and 1 of **butter**—about tablespoon **flour** and 3 or 4 tablespoons of **milk**. **2 eggs** will make about 1 pie.

Charlotte Russe

½ box Knox® gelatine soaked in ½ cup cold water,
dissolved in 1 cup of boiling water
To this, add 1 cup of sugar
After this cools and begins to thicken, beat in the **whites of 4 eggs**, beaten stiff

Last, beat in **1 pint of cream beaten stiff** (or as much cream as you have.)

Mari Ana Pemble Davis said, "Oh, Charlotte Russe was always served on Christmas with just a dash of bourbon cooked in it. Almost everybody served it at Christmas along with fruitcake. It was a little more congealed than boiled custard, and it was served cold."

Jam Cake

Cream 1 cup sugar
½ cup butter
Add yolks of 4 eggs, beat
3 cups flour
Heaping teaspoon baking powder
½ teaspoon soda
2 tablespoons clabber or ½ cup buttermilk
1 cup jam
1 teaspoon cloves
1 teaspoon spice
Beat well, then add whites of 4 eggs.

Spiced Nut Cake

½ cup butter

1 cup brown sugar

½ cup molasses

Yolk of 4 eggs

1 cup of sour milk

2 ½ cups flour

1 teaspoon soda

1 ½ cups baking powder

1 teaspoon each of cinnamon, spice, cloves

1 cup seeded raisins

½ cup currants

¾ cup English walnuts

Cream butter; add sugar slowly. Add molasses, eggs beaten light; stir 2 cups flour with soda, baking powder and spices. Add alternately with milk. Roll fruit with rest of flour.

Cup Cake

4 eggs

2 cups sugar

3 cups flour

1 cup water

2 teaspoons baking powder

½ cup butter

Fruit Cake

3 cups sugar

1 cup butter

6 eggs

5 cups flour

1 cup sweet milk

2 teaspoons baking powder

2 spoons spice

2 spoons cloves

2 spoons nutmeg powdered

2 spoons cinnamon

3 or 4 lbs. raisins, seeded

2 lbs. currants

5 cts. Citron or watermelon rind (1 /2 cup) preserves

1 cup molasses with scant teaspoon soda

Cup whiskey

If you like nuts, add about 2 cups.

Icing

2 teacups sugar

½ teacup water

Let boil till spins thread. Beat whites of 2 eggs stiff and beat into as divinity.

Cocoanut Filling

1 cup milk

¾ cup sugar

Add **whole grated cocoanut**. Boil till milk gets thick looking. Spread on cake.

Buttermilk Pie

2 eggs

¾ cup sugar

Lump butter

1 tablespoon flour

1 cup buttermilk

Flavor to taste with spice, vanilla, or lemon as preferred.

Put in a crust and bake slowly.

Cream Pie

Make Cream Pie same way as Buttermilk Pie, only substitute sweet milk for buttermilk.

Chili Sauce

12 large tomatoes

2 large onions

2 green peppers

2 cups vinegar

¾ cup sugar

Tablespoon cinnamon

Tablespoon salt

Let boil till thick, if not sweet enough, add more sugar. If it takes too long to thicken, wet a little flour in vinegar and stir in.

---

*In addition to her favorite recipes from her mother, Bess gleaned a recipe from **Joe Stewart** who had become a close friend while they were at Mississippi State College for Women. It is written in Joe's hand. She may have attended the shower and written it then, or added it later:*

French Gumbo

1 large onion
1 can of tomatoes
1can of okra or 1 qt. fresh okra
1 large slice ham
1 lb. beef
1 chicken
1 can shrimp or 1 lb. fresh shrimp
1 can oyster or 2 dozen fresh oysters
1 can crabs or 1 dozen fresh crabs
1 pod red pepper
½ teaspoon black pepper
Salt to taste

Fry onion (chopped fine) to light brown. Add tomatoes and stew until well done. Add okra (cut into small pieces) and stew until okra falls to pieces. Grind meat and fry it and cut up chicken. Add this to tomatoes and okra. Add 2 quarts of water and boil for 2 hours very slowly. Add oysters, shrimp and crabs ½ hour before time to serve. Serve over boiled rice. This will serve 12 people.

---

*Bess and Ed Rayner lived with the **John S. Finchers** for a few months after their marriage. Bess collected several recipes from Mrs. Fincher in addition to the one that Mrs. Fincher included in the initial collection. Mrs. Fincher's great-granddaughter, Sandy Speakes Huerta is now a proprietor of one of the most successful restaurants in Cleveland at the Warehouse.*

Mince Meat

1 peck green tomatoes

1½ cups vinegar

5 lbs. sugar

2 lemon rinds and juice

2 tablespoons allspice

2 tablespoons cinnamon

2 tablespoons cloves

2 tablespoons salt

2 lbs. prunes, stoned and chopped

3 lbs. raisins, seeded and chopped

Run all this through food chopper, (except vinegar, salt and sugar); spices are in powdered form and are added when put on stove to heat before sealing. Two lbs. of dried apples may be added to increase quantity; if so, cook before adding to mixture.

Pineapple Sherbet

1 quart milk

1 can grated pineapple

3 or 4 lemons

Whites of 3 eggs

Sweeten lemon and pineapple to taste and fold the egg whites into milk after it has been chilled. Freeze [in crank ice cream freezer]. Makes about 3 quarts.

Oatmeal Cookies

1 cup sugar

1 cup shortening

2 eggs

1 cup buttermilk

1 teaspoon soda

Dash salt

1 cup raisins

2 tablespoons cocoa

1 teaspoon cinnamon

1 teaspoon allspice

2 cups flour

2 cups oatmeal

1 cup nuts

Mix together into a dough. If dough seems too soft, add little more flour. Drop by spoon on greased tin. Bake in moderate oven.

Lemon Sauce

(Mrs. Fincher served with plain sponge cake)

1-cup sugar
3 level tablespoons flour
2 cups boil water
2 teaspoons lemon juice

Mix flour and sugar. Add water, boil till thick. Then add **lump of butter**.

Caramel Filling

3 cups sugar
1 cup milk

Brown ½ of the sugar and pour in to other half that's boiling with milk.

Another contributor to the Rayner recipe collection was **Lizbeth (Mrs. Sam) Field**, Bess' sister-in-law. These are hers:

Celia's Hot Tamales

1 large onion, chopped and fried brown
1 can tomatoes
2 cups or 1 lb. chopped meat, browned
1 tablespoon or more Mexine®
Salt and pepper to taste
1 tablespoon sugar
½ lb. spaghetti, cooked with butter, *or* corn meal

Layer spaghetti or corn meal and layer of tamale mixture. Repeat and sprinkle with American cheese on top. Run in oven and bake.

Meat Loaf

1 # ground round steak
Onions chopped fine
Celery
Lemon juice
Salt, pepper, parsley

Roll in **toast crumbs**. Brown on top of stove in iron skillet with **bacon grease**. Cook slowly in moderate oven basting frequently.

Waffles

1 cup sifted flour
1 cup buttermilk
¼ cup Wesson® oil
1 teaspoon salt
1 teaspoon baking powder
½ teaspoon soda

Mix in dry ingredients and beat egg in milk; add oil. If you use sweet milk (better) use no soda.

Millionaire Pie

1 ½ cups sugar
3 eggs
2 tablespoons vinegar
2 tablespoons water
2 tablespoons melted butter
1 teaspoon cinnamon
2/3 cup pecans
2/3 cup raisins

Bake in muffin pans. Cut crust with lid of 1# coffee can. Makes 17 pies. [Coffee can lids in this time were metal and were removed by a key and twist system, leaving a sharp edge perfect for cutting these crusts.]

Another important contributor to the cookbook in her own hand, was "E Loys" who was **Emma Loys Steidley McLaurin**, originally from Crawley, Louisiana, and the wife of J. Purves McLaurin, Sr. and mother of Dr. Purves McLaurin of Oxford. Like the Pembles and the Fields, the McLaurins had known each other in south Mississippi before they came to Merigold. Mr. McLaurin was from Woodville near Centreville. According to Latham, "She was here in the Methodist church, lived over near where we lived when Cack and I were growing up. And she and Mother were real good friends. She boarded schoolteachers. They lived in what we called 'the high-up house.' It's where the Johnsons live now who teach at the college. It's a two-story house right on the bank of the bayou and it's a Sears Roebuck house. Now you may not be familiar with a Sears Roebuck house."

Pictured at right are Bess Rayner (left) with her friend E. Loys at a "costume event" dressed as women did in the 1930s. This was at a United Methodist Women meeting at the Rayner home in 1973.

The following recipes are from Emma Loys:

Barbecued Chicken

Split **1 chicken** down back. Put on in pan with **2 cups hot water** and cook 30 minutes in oven. Then pour following ingredients mixed together to make a sauce:

> 8 tablespoons tomato catsup
> 2 tablespoons vinegar
> 2 tablespoons lemon juice or ½ lemon
> 2 tablespoons Worcestershire sauce
> 2 tablespoons butter
> 3 drops of Tabasco sauce

Cook until tender.

Prune Whip

1 cup prune pulp

3 egg whites, beaten until stiff

3 tablespoons sugar

1 teaspoon vanilla

½ cup chopped nuts

Mix egg whites, sugar and vanilla and fold into prune pulp. Add nuts and pout into greased dish. Set this in a pan of hot water and bake in medium oven.

Strawberry Preserves

2 quarts strawberries (chopped) placed in colander, then pour 2 quarts hot water over berries. Drain. Place in boiler and put over them 1 quart sugar . Come to a boil and boil for 5 minutes. Then put in 1 quart sugar and boil again for 15 minutes. Set off to get cold, then put in jars.

Tiffs

3 egg whites

1/8 teaspoon salt

9 tablespoons sugar

½ teaspoon vanilla

1 cup nuts

Mix and bake in oven at 300 for 25 minutes.

Oatmeal Cookies

2 eggs

1 cup sugar

1 cup lard and butter mix

Dissolve 12 teaspoons soda in 10 teaspoons sweet milk

1 cup chopped raisins or ½ cup nuts

1 level teaspoon cinnamon

2 cups flour

2 cups uncooked coarse oatmeal

Grease pan. Drop 1 teaspoonful at a time not to touch.

Ellie Jeter was a fellow schoolteacher in Merigold. These recipes were gathered by Bess Rayner from her collection:

Rice Croquettes

1 pt. cooked rice
2 or 3 tablespoons milk
3 tablespoons butter
½ teaspoon salt
White pepper
Cayenne
1 egg
2 teaspoons chopped parsley

Warm rice in double boiler with enough milk to moisten it. Add butter, seasoning, and beaten egg and cook until egg thickens. Spread mixture on a plate. When cool, shape into cylinders. Dip in **dried bread crumbs, egg** and dried bread crumbs again. Cook in **deep hot fat.**

Lemon Pie

1 heaping tablespoon cornstarch
1 cup sugar
1 cup fruit juice
1 lemon rind, grated
2 egg yolks
1 cup boiling water
Little salt
1 tablespoon butter

Pineapple Pie

Substitute pineapple for above lemon juice. Cut down on boiling water

Cheese Pudding

1 cup grated cheese
1 cup milk
¼ cup dried breadcrumbs
1 egg
½ teaspoon salt
Cayenne

Beat egg slightly and add other ingredients. Turn into buttered baking dish, custard cups or ramekins. Place in pan of hot water and bake in a moderate oven until the mixture is firm. Serve hot.

Molasses Pie

1 cup sugar
1 cup molasses
1 cup milk
3 egg yolks
3 heaping tablespoons cornstarch
Butter size of walnut

Five Threes

3 pints water
3 ¼ cupfuls sugar
3 lemons
3 oranges
3 bananas

Make syrup of sugar and water, then cool it. Extract the juice from lemons and oranges; crush the peeled and scraped bananas with wooden potato masher. Mix fruits at once with syrup. Freeze at once.

Bess Rayner's sister-in-law, **Thelma Rayner** *was the wife of E. D. Rayner's brother Ira. Sue Rayner Latham recalled, "They lived down near Rolling Fork. Uncle Ike farmed down there and the flood came. They were living at Fitler when the 1927 flood came. I think maybe that's when they came here. I'm not really sure. But anyway, Uncle Ike farmed." They had three children: Benny who died in an auto accident as a child, Allen, who is not living now, and Clay. Thelma was a native of Port Gibson, Mississippi. She loved reading and was instrumental in founding Bolivar County's first public library in Merigold in 1934. She worked tirelessly as a volunteer librarian and today it is named in her memory. The Ira Rayners built a beautiful house on old Highway 61 in Merigold next door to his brother E. D. Rayner's home. In the house, they used moldings, doors, windows, and mantels from the old family home ins Fitler. The Ira Rayner house still stands today. Bess collected these recipes from Thelma in the 1930s:*

Thelma's Salad

1 pkg. lemon gelatin

2 cups boiling water

1 teaspoon salt

Pepper to taste

1 cup celery

1 cup pecans

1 small can pimento

1 large apple

Mix all ingredients and refrigerate until congealed.

Bread and Butter Pickle

12 large cucumbers

2 large onions

Soak in brine 3 hours. Drain.

2 cups vinegar

2 cups sugar

1 teaspoon each of celery seed, mustard seed and turmeric.

Bring to boil add vegetables and let come to rolling boil. Seal.

Cranberry Tarts

3 cups berries

1 ½ cups sugar

1 cup boiling water

Mix these ingredients and boil for 10 minutes. Pour into baked pastry shells in muffin pans.

*Bess Rayner's sister **Eva Field Beckham** settled in Shaw. She gave Bess these recipes for her book:*

Imperial Salad

Draw juice from **half can of pineapple**; add **1 tablespoon of vinegar** and enough water to make a pint. Heat to boiling point and add **one pkg. lemon Jell-O®**. Just as Jell-O® begins to set, add **3 slices of canned pineapple**, cubed, and **one-half can pimento** shredded. Mould in individual or 1 large mould and slice. Serve with **cream salad dressing.**

Golden Glow Salad

1 Lemon Jell-O®
1 cup boiling water
1 cup pineapple juice
1 tablespoon vinegar

Mix and refrigerate. When it begins to congeal, put in **1 cup diced pineapple** and **1 cup grated carrots.**

Lemon Pie

2 lemons
½ cup sugar
6 eggs
1 tablespoon butter
Flour
½ cup sweet milk

Save out whites of 4 eggs and add 4 tablespoons sugar for meringue.

Apple Betty

4 tart apples
1 cup soft bread crumbs
1 cup Baker's® coconut
1 cup brown sugar
1 teaspoon cinnamon
4 tablespoons butter

Arrange layers of apples in greased baking dish. Cover with bread crumbs and coconut. Sprinkle with sugar and cinnamon. Dot with butter. Repeat. Bake in 350 degree oven for 30 minutes, covered. Uncover and bake for 10 minutes until apples are soft. Pecans sprinkled in are good.

These recipes were collected from her sister-in-law **Mary Field**, *who was the wife of Dr. C. L. Field of Shaw*:

White Salad

> 1 pint cream, whipped
> 1 envelope gelatin, dissolved in cold water
> ½ cup boiling water, or pineapple juice with lemon
> 1 ½ box marshmallows, cut
> 1 can pineapple
> 1 cup nuts (pecans or almonds)

To whipped cream, add 1 cup of cooked dressing

> <u>Cooked Dressing:</u>
> 3 egg yolks to ½ cup sugar
> 1 scant tablespoon flour

Have **1 cup vinegar and ½ cup water boiling**. Mix and add **pinch of butter the size of an egg.** [Sue and Cack say that Aunt Mary thought everything needed a little cooked dressing on it and she used it on her congealed salads and on her chicken salad.]

Congealed Cranberry Salad

> 1 package lemon Jell-O® dissolved in 1 cup boiling water
> 2 cups sugar
> 1 cup of water
> 4 cups of cranberries
> 1 cup chopped celery
> 1 cup chopped pineapple
> Juice of 1 lemon

Mix all ingredients and congeal.

Pineapple-Cheese Salad

1 #2-can crushed pineapple

¾ cup sugar

Juice of 1 lemon

Pinch salt

2 envelopes gelatin

1 cup grated cheese

1 cup cream, whipped

Mix together the pineapple, sugar, lemon juice, and salt. Let come to boil, and then add gelatin previously soaked in 1-cup cold water. Beat vigorously and when beginning to set, add cheese and cream. Put in cool place to congeal. Add pimento to ¼ cup of celery if liked.

Cheese Straws

1 cup grated cheese

1-teaspoon baking powder

1-½ cups flour

2 tablespoons melted butter

Pinch salt

Pinch cayenne pepper

Enough milk to mix and roll

Mix, cut or press, and bake in a quick oven.

In addition, Bess Rayner collected recipes from these cooks:

Chicken Spaghetti

1 hen, cooked and cut, de-boned, and chopped

1 lb. spaghetti

1 can mushroom soup

1 stalk celery (1 ½ cup)

1 green pepper

2 medium onions

1 large can broken mushrooms

Cream, butter, salt, and pepper to taste

Brown celery, onions, and pepper in butter. Add mushrooms and soup. Thicken if needed. Add cooked spaghetti and chopped chicken.

Margaret Saunders

Mrs. Saunders husband taught school at Merigold. They later moved to Columbus.

English Pie

4 eggs, beaten separately
2 cup s sugar
1 lump butter the size of egg, or ½ cup cream
1 cup raisins
1 cup nuts
1 teaspoon each nutmeg, cinnamon, and cloves
1 tablespoon vinegar
1 teaspoon vanilla

Mix all ingredients, folding in egg whites first. Pour into an unbaked crust and bake in medium oven.

Ethlyn Speakes

Ethlyn Speakes was the daughter of Mr. and Mrs. John S. Fincher and the wife of Harry Speakes who had a store in downtown Merigold. They lived in a house facing the park near the Methodist Church still owned today by their son Larry Speakes, former press secretary to President Ronald Reagan.

Cherry Cocoanut Mold

1 pkg. Sweetened cherry gelatin
1 cup hot water
1 cup ice and water
1 cup whipping cream
11/2 cups lightly sweetened grated cocoanut
¼ cup sliced maraschino cherries

Pour the hot water over the gelatin and when it has melted, add ice cubes to water. When ice has melted, place in refrigerator until slightly thickened. Beat with electric beater until air bubbles are small, fold in sliced cherries and cocoanut, and finally fold in cream, which has been whipped until thick.

Mrs. Young

Lillian Young was the wife of Mr. Fred Young, the Merigold School superintendent, who served the area for over twenty-five years until 1945. She is remembered as being "very proper."

French Dressing

Equal parts of vinegar and oil
½ teaspoon Worcestershire sauce
½ teaspoon salt
Dash paprika
1 teaspoon catsup
1 hard-boiled egg yolk, put through sieve
Chopped parsley
Pepper to taste

Big Sis (Claire Marx)

Big Sis' Cocoanut Candy

2/3 cup milk

2 cups sugar

Put on stove and cook until sugar melts. Put in **1 cup fresh cocoanut** and cook until it thickens. Take out small amount and beat till stiff and drop on wet board in mounds.

Chicken Croquettes

2 cups chicken, cut very fine
1 heaping tablespoon butter
2 heaping tablespoons flour
1 cup sweet milk
2 teaspoons onion juice
2 pieces celery, cut fine

Melt butter in saucepan; add flour; stir well. Add milk, onion juice, celery, and continue to stir. Cook until thick. Add **salt and pepper** to taste. Add chicken and place in ice box for 1 hour. Roll plenty of **crackers** into crumbs. Beat **2 eggs**. Add to each **1 table-spoon water**. Roll croquettes in crumbs, then dip in egg. Roll again and shape into cones. Fry in deep **fat**. Makes about 12.

Auntie (Bell)

Corn Relish

18 large ears of tender corn

6 large onions

11 green peppers—hot

1 head of cabbage (Mr. R. Leaves this out)

1 red pepper, hot

12 bell peppers

½ box Coleman's® mustard

½ tea cup salt

2 # brown sugar

1 ½ teaspoons turmeric

2 quarts vinegar

Cook until pepper turns brown.

Mr. Rickles

Ice Box Pie

2 ½ lemons

2 egg yolks

2 tablespoons sugar

1 can Dime® brand condensed milk

Pie crust

Anna (Aunt Mildred Field's cook)

These next recipes were collected by Bess Rayner from **Cakie Robinson Field** *of Centreville*

Peach Cream

1 quart peaches

1 cup cream, whipped

1 cup water

1 tablespoon granulated gelatin

2/3 cup sugar

¼ cup cold water

Cook peaches till tender with water and sugar, then pass thru sieve. Soak gelatin for 10 minutes in ¼ cup water; then heat to boiling point and add to peaches. Whip cream stiff and add to fruit pulp when latter is nearly cold. Mix smoothly and turn into a china or granite mould. Have cream very cold when turned out. The mould may be decorated with fresh peaches if desired. Canned peaches may be used for making this dessert.

Ice Cream

Fill freezer ¾ full with **milk and cream** and **1 pkg. gelatine**. **Sugar** to taste. Add fruit if desired.

Cream Biscuit or Cakes

1 egg
1 scant cup flour
1 scant cup milk or cream (sweet)
1 scant teaspoon baking powder
1 tablespoon butter, unless cream is used—then use teaspoon butter

Butter Fingers

7/8 cup shortening
5 tablespoons sugar
1 teaspoon vanilla
2 cups flour
1 tablespoon water
1 cup nuts, chopped

Cream shortening and sugar. Add vanilla. Add flour gradually and beat after each addition. Add water and nut meats of any preferred kind. Shape into oblong cookies about the size of a finger. Bake in a moderate oven (350 degrees F) 15 to 20 minutes. When cool, roll each cookie in granulated sugar. This makes about 3-dozen.

Sara George Smith (Mrs. James R. Smith, Jr.)

Sara George Smith came from Okolona, Mississippi in the hills. Her mother's name was Sara and her father's name was George, so she was named Sara George. She was married to James Roger Smith, Jr. the son of "Big Daddy" and she was the mother of Jimmy Smith and grandmother of Jamie and Stephen Smith who are connected today with McCarty's.

Frozen Fruit Cake

2 cups milk
½ cup sugar
¼ cup flour
¼ teaspoon salt
2 eggs
1 teaspoon vanilla
1 cup white raisins
1 cup broken pecans
2 cups crumbled macaroons
½ cup chopped candied cherries
1 cup cream, whipped

Scald milk. Blend sugar, flour, salt, add to milk. Stir until smooth. Cook 10 minutes. Pour over beaten eggs, cook until thick stirring constantly. Cool. Add other ingredients, folding in the whipping cream last. Freeze in tins.

Sarah George Smith

Corn Flake Cookies

4 whites, beaten stiff
1 cup sugar
1 ½ cup nuts
3 cups corn flakes
1 cup cocoanut

Beat sugar into egg whites. Add nuts, cereal and cocoanut. Drop out and bake in moderate oven for 4 to 5 minutes.

Mrs. Gilbert

Angel Food Cake

11 whites, beat till frothy, add **1 teaspoon cream tartar**, beat with same stroke till stiff. Add slowly **1 ½ cups sugar**. Add **extract**. Add **1 cup flour** sift well and measured. Then sift four times, bake slow.

Icing

1 ¾ cups sugar
¾ cup cold water, let boil till forms ball in water. Pour.

Mrs. Malley

Mrs. W. L. Malley *had a little store on South Street and was known for her delicious cakes.*

Ice Box Rolls

1 qt. sweet milk
1 cup sugar
1 cup lard
1 cake of yeast
1 teaspoon soda, rounded
1 heaping teaspoon baking powder
2 teaspoons salt

Scald milk, add sugar and lard and set aside to get lukewarm. Then add yeast which has been dissolved in warm water. Add enough flour to make about as stiff as cake batter. Let rise about 3 hours or until a little more than double in bulk, or depends on temperature of kitchen and weather. Then add baking powder and salt and soda. And work in enough flour to make dough. Roll and cut as many rolls as you want and let rise about 2 hours. Put the rest of dough in ice box and use as desired. Always allow about 2 hours to rise before baking.

Mrs. Broom

Roll Variations Clover Leaf—Put 3 small balls of dough in muffin pans.
Twin Rolls—Put 2 small balls of dough in muffing pan.
Pan Rolls—Place balls of dough almost touching each other in square or round pans
Finger Rolls—Using the palms of the hands, make long thin fingers; place an inch apart on the pan.
Braided Rolls—Take 3 long thin rolls of dough, braid them in the usual way. Snip them with scissors at the desired length. Brush with egg white and sprinkle with poppy seeds.
Whole Wheat Rolls—Substitute 3 cups of whole wheat flour for white flour
Bran Rolls—Add 1 cup of cooking bran
Fruit Rolls—2 cupfuls of ground raisin, figs, dates, nuts, or any of these in combination added to plain white, whole wheat, or bran recipe.
Walnut Date Tea Biscuits—Stuff dates with halves of English walnuts . Cover with thin coating of basic dough and let rise in usual manner. Excellent with fruit salad.

—from a clipping attached to the above recipe by Mrs. E. D. Rayner

Devil's Food

2 scant cups sugar

½ cup butter

4 eggs

1 cup sweet milk

2 ¼ cups flour

1 square baker's chocolate

1 teaspoon cream of tartar

½ teaspoon soda

1 teaspoon soda

1 teaspoon vanilla

½ teaspoon allspice

½ teaspoon cloves

½ teaspoon cinnamon

Cream butter; add half sugar, beat yolks lightly. Mix butter and yolk. Add remainder of sugar. Add milk slowly thru flour. (Sift flour and soda 5 times) Add melted chocolate, beat whites, add cream tartar and then add whites to cake.

Mrs. Broom

Lady Baltimore

3 ½ cups sugar

2 teaspoons baking powder

2 cups sugar

1 cup butter

6 egg whites

1 cup milk

Mrs. Broom

Chocolate Fudge Cake

¼ # [lb.] butter or half cup
1 cup sugar
1 cup flour
1 cup pecans
1 1/8 of a cake of bitter chocolate
2 eggs
Vanilla flavoring

Melt chocolate and butter. Beat eggs and sugar. Mix flour and pecans.

Icing

2 cups of pulverized sugar
2 tablespoon cocoa mix together
1 tablespoon of butter

Use sweet milk or cream until the right consistency to spread. Best to put your icing where is will get a little warm to get the butter well blended; beat till smooth.

Mrs. Robinson

Up Side Down Pineapple Cake

Melt **1/8 # butter and 1 ½ cup brown sugar** in iron skillet. Let cool and cover bottom of skillet with **sliced pineapple**. Fill holes with **pecans and chopped cherries**. Cream **1/3 cup butter and 1 cup sugar**. Add beaten **yolk of 1 egg**, **¾ cup sweet milk**, **1 ¾ cups flour**, **4 teaspoons baking powder**, **and 1 teaspoon vanilla**.

Locke

Mrs. Charlie Locke *was the former Ruth Calhoun, Mari Ana Pemble Davis' aunt. The ladies' class at the Baptist church in Merigold was named for her.*

Mustard Pickle

1 gallon sliced cucumbers
1 gallon sliced green tomatoes
1 gallon sliced onions
Celery seed, if liked
2 small size cans mustard
2 cups sugar
12 tablespoons flour
4 tablespoons turmeric

Slice vegetables fine and dredge with salt. Let stand for several hours, drain. Place contents on stove, add sufficient vinegar to cover. Let come to a boil. Stir in paste. Let cook till thick, stirring constantly to prevent sticking. Mix mustard in hot water to keep from lumping.

Miss Nenie Crawford (from Centreville)

Chili Sauce

1 gallon ripe tomatoes
1 gallon cabbage
1 gallon onions
1 cup salt

Chop vegetables fine, sprinkle with **salt**. Let stand for 2 hours. Drain. Then add **½ gallon vinegar, 3 # sugar (6 cups), spices to taste, and 12 large green peppers chopped fine**. Cook 30 minutes. This makes 12 pints and its grand.

[Bess Rayner added, "Going by this recipe, I made 1 ½ measure and made 18 pints in 1931. (Don't <u>drain too dry</u>.)"]

Miss Nenie Crawford

Date Loaf

3 cups of sugar
1 cup milk

Boil together till you can form soft ball in water. Put in **package of dates** and cook to form ball. It won't stick to your fingers. Take from fire, put in cup pecans, and beat until nearly cold. Add pinch of **salt and flavoring**. Pour on wet cloth and roll.

Miss Manese

Several recipes were written down by Mrs. Rayner without a reference to their sources. Many appear to have been used over and over again as her standard instructions for basic things such as fudge, peanut brittle, pie pastry and breakfast cocoa.

Cocoa Syrup

½ cup Baker's Breakfast Cocoa®
1-cup water
1 1/2 cups sugar
Dash salt
2 teaspoons vanilla

Over direct heat, stir the cocoa and water until smooth. Stir in sugar and salt until dissolved. Boil for 3 minutes and then add vanilla. Pour in a glass jar, seal it and keep it in the ice chest.

Sue Rayner Latham said, "Now this recipe I use every time I need it. Mother made our own chocolate syrup. We didn't know you could buy it. But anyway, it's a good recipe. You make cold cocoa, hot chocolate, syrup on ice cream—any way you wanted to use it.

Cack Rayner Meyer added, " I remember Mother used that all the time. We had our own cow so Mother had plenty of milk."

Twenty Four Hour Salad

¼ cupful sugar
2 tablespoons flour
¼ teaspoon salt
2 egg yolks
1/3 cupful lemon juice
1/3 cupful pineapple juice
½ cupful of whipping cream
1 cupful diced pineapple
1 cupful seeded white cherries
1 cupful diced marshmallow
½ cupful of blanched and shredded almonds

Blend together the sugar, the flour and the salt in the double boiler. Add the fruit juices and the boil over hot water and cook until very thick . And add the cream whipped. Drain the fruit, marshmallows, and nut meats, combine with cooked mixture and place in refrigerator for 24 hours. At serving time, place the particles of fruit, marshmallows, and nuts on individual plates and serve cold.

Cream Cheese Salad

1 pkg. Lemon Jell-O®
Juice of 1 can pineapple

Heat juice to boiling point and add Jell-O®. Place aside to cool. Then beat with rotary egg beater till it begins to thicken. Have **2 packages cream cheese** mashed soft and add to **1 cup cream, whipped.** Then add to cream the Jell-O and **1 cup nuts, ½ cup celery, 1 cup crushed pineapple, 1 large pimiento, and fine salt and pepper to taste.** Mold.

Jellied Chicken Salad

1 package lemon flavored gelatin mixture
2 cups boiling water
2 tablespoons lemon juice
1 cup diced, cooked chicken
½ cup diced celery
2 tablespoons chopped pimientos
½ teaspoon salt
1/4 teaspoon paprika
1 cup stiff mayonnaise

Pour water over gelatin mixture and stir until it has dissolved. Cool and allow to thicken a little. Add the lemon juice, chicken, celery, pimientos, salt and paprika. Pour into individual molds and chill until stiff. Unmold in crisp lettuce cups and top with mayonnaise.

Perfection Salad

1 package Lemon or Lime Jell-O®
1 pint boiling water
2 tablespoons vinegar
½ teaspoon salt
½ cup cabbage, finely shredded
1 cup celery, finely cut
1 pimiento, finely cut
1 tablespoon green pepper, finely chopped

Dissolve Jell-O® in boiling water. Add vinegar and salt. Chill. When slightly thickened, fold in cabbage, celery, pimiento, and green pepper. Turn into individual molds. Chill until firm. Unmold on crisp lettuce. Garnish with Hellmann's® mayonnaise. Serves 6.

Tuna Fish Salad

½ envelope Knox Acidulated Gelatine®
¼ cup cold water
1 cup tuna fish
½ green pepper, finely chopped
2 tablespoonfuls chopped olives
½ cup chopped celery
¾ cup boiled salad dressing
½ teaspoonful salt
¼ teaspoonful paprika
Few grains cayenne

Soak gelatine in cold water five minutes, and add to hot boiled salad dressing. Cook and add tuna fish, separated into flakes, celery, pepper (from which seeds have been removed), olives, salt, paprika, cayenne, ¼ teaspoonful Lemon Flavoring found in separate envelope. Dissolved in two teaspoonfuls water. Turn into six individual molds, or a larger mold, first dipped in cold water, and chill. Remove from molds to nests of lettuce leaves, and garnish with slices cut from pimolas, diamond shaped pieces cut from green peppers, celery tip's and watercress. (Obviously taken from a Knox Gelatine® recipe folder.)

Savory Cheese Salad

2 teaspoonfuls Knox Sparkling Gelatine®
¼ cup cold water
½ cup boiling water
½ teaspoonful salt
¼ cup vinegar
1 ½ cups grated cheese
½ cup stuffed olives, chopped
½ cup celery, chopped
¼ cup green pepper, chopped
½ cup cream or evaporated milk, whipped

Soak gelatine in cold water about 5 minutes. Dissolve in boiling water; add salt and vinegar. When nearly set, beat until frothy, fold in cheese, olives, celery, pepper, and whipped cream. Chill until firma and unmold on lettuce leaves. Serve with salad dressing.

Oyster Patties

(10 Patties)

3 tablespoons butter

1 teaspoon lemon juice

2 tablespoons flour

Salt and pepper or cayenne

½ cup cream

1 cup solid oysters

½ cup oyster liquor

Puff pastry patty shells

Blend butter and flour in saucepan, add cream and oyster liquor, stir till boiling and cook slowly 5 minutes longer. Free oysters from bits of shell and scald in their own liquor and add to the hot sauce, together with the seasonings. Bring almost to boiling point and fill shells. Serve hot.

Chicken Patties

Prepare same as oyster patties, substitute chicken liquor for oyster and sliced chicken for oysters. A little grated lemon rind may also be substitutes for lemon juice.

Chicken Croquettes with White Sauce

(This recipe was cut out of Crisco promotional literature and includes an artist's rendering of the croquettes glued with the recipe.)

2 cupfuls cooked chicken

½ teaspoonful salt

¼ teaspoonful celery salt (if desired)

1 teaspoonful lemon juice

1/2 teaspoonful scraped onion

1 cupful white sauce

Mix the ingredients is the order given. Cool the mixture. Roll in beaten eggs, then crumbs and fry in hot Crisco.

<u>White sauce</u>

2 tablespoonfuls Crisco®

4 tablespoonfuls flour

1 cupful milk

Salt and pepper to taste

Melt Crisco; add flour, stirring to a smooth paste. Then add milk gradually. Stir over the fire until smooth and thick. In frying the croquettes use sufficient Crisco® to fill the kettle about 2/3 full. (We suggest that you order 3 pounds.) Put the Crisco® in a cold kettle and heat it gradually until a crumb of bread dropped into it becomes a golden brown in 40 seconds. Notice that Crisco® does not sputter or boil over when the croquettes are dropped into it. That is because it contains no moisture.

Chicken Loaf

1 chicken
12 eggs
2 small envelopes of gelatine
Chicken stock

Separate white and dark meat. Also, yolks and whites of eggs. Dissolve gelatine in cup of cold stock. Then add 4 cups stock hot. Pour some of this over each of ingredients until they are quite moist. Put moistened white meat in bottom of pan, and then yolks; then dark meat then whites of eggs. Press firm. Slice and serve cold. Celery may be added to white meat and nuts to dark meat.

Meat Balls

1 pound of ground steak
1 onion, grated
A little parsley chopped fine
1 egg
½ cup bread crumbs
Lump of butter
Salt and pepper
A little garlic, if liked

Mix meat and the egg (slightly beaten) with all of the other ingredients. Shape into round balls, sprinkle with flour and fry in hot fat. When done, remove from skillet and add to the grease about a teaspoon of flour and make a very thin gravy. To this add half of a very small can of tomato paste, or a small can of tomatoes. Put the meat balls into this and let simmer for about half an hour. Nice to serve over noodles or macaroni.

Oysters on Half Shell with Cocktail Sauce

24 oysters on half shell

4 lemons

Mix together:

2 tablespoons tomato catsup

12 drops Tabasco sauce

3 tablespoons lemon juice

Salt

1 tablespoon finely chopped onion

½ teaspoon grated horseradish

Cut two sections from each lemon and remove juice and pulp, leaving baskets with handles. Mix lemon juice with other seasonings, adding salt to taste. Put mixture in baskets and place each one in center of a deep plate of crushed ice. Arrange six oysters around each basket and serve for a first course.

Fried Oysters

Use **large oysters** and look them over carefully for bits of shell. Wash and then roll in **highly seasoned corn flour**. Let dry 10 minutes, then dip in **prepared egg**, then roll in **fine breadcrumbs**. Stand aside to dry 10 minutes. Have **fat** sufficiently hot, about 370 degrees F. Fry only three at once to keep from reducing the temperature of the fat.

The seasoned corn flour:

1 cup corn flour

2 teaspoons salt

1 ½ teaspoons paprika.

Sift three times.

To prepare the egg dip:

1 egg

6 tablespoons oyster liquid

1 tablespoon Worcester sauce

1 teaspoon salt

1 teaspoon paprika, 1 tablespoon grated onion

Beat well to mix and then use.

Bread Crumbs:

Put dried bread thru the food chopper and then sift and sort until needed.

Boiled Eggs with Cream Sauce

Hard boil the desired number of eggs. Arrange in bowl and pour over them the following sauce:

<u>Sauce for 6 Eggs</u>

1 ½ cups sweet milk, heated to boiling

Thicken with 2 tablespoons flour made to paste

When of the consistency of thick cream, add **one cup grated cheese**

Beat well and pour over eggs. (Fine for emergencies.)

Cooked Mayonnaise

Into mixing bowl put **yolks of 2 eggs, 1 teaspoon salt, ½ teaspoon mustard, 2 tablespoons lemon juice, 2 tablespoons vinegar, and 1 cup oil.** Do not stir. Have ready a sauce made of **1 cup water, 1 tablespoon butter, 1/3 cup flour.** Cook this about 10 minutes in a double boiler and turn sauce hot into bowl containing other ingredients and beat well with eggbeater.

Cucumber Pickle

1 gallon vinegar come to boil

1 cup salt

1 cup sugar

Spices to taste

1 teaspoon alum in vinegar

Take cucumbers cut in small pieces. Put layer of cucumbers, few **green tomatoes**, few **whole onions**, bean, pinch **hot pepper**, few **spices**, then another layer, then pour hot vinegar with ingredients. Cover jar.

Pepper Hash

12 green peppers

2 tablespoons salt

12 small onions cut fine

1 ½ cups vinegar

12 red peppers

1 ½ tablespoon celery seed

1 ½ cups sugar

Put on in boiling water, Set on back of stove, let simmer, cook until done, little longer than 10 minutes.

Peach Pickle

To 1 pint of fruit use ½ of that amount of sugar. To 10 # sugar, use 1 quart of vinegar, (Heinz® pickling). *(With this amount of sugar and vinegar I used just plain vinegar, too.) I pickled about a bushel of peaches and it made 13 quarts pickles—8/1/1930.)*

Let sugar and vinegar come to a good boil. Drop in peaches a few at a time and cook until can pierce with a fork. Place in jars with whole spice and cloves (about 8 each to quart jar) and pour bubbly syrup over.

Chocolate Fudge

3 cups Granulated Sugar
2 tablespoons Cocoa
1 tablespoon Mazola®
¾ cup Milk
1 teaspoon Vanilla
½ teaspoon Salt
2 tablespoons, Karo, Blue Label®

Cook together sugar, cocoa, Karo, Mazola, salt and milk until it forms a soft ball when dropped in cold water. Set aside until cool. Add vanilla and beat until it creams. Pour into oiled pan and cut in squares.

Peanut Brittle

1 cup Karo, Blue Label®
1 cup Brown Sugar
2 tablespoons Water
1 cup Shelled Peanuts
2 teaspoons Mazola®

Boil sugar, Karo and water until it is crisp when dropped in cold water. Just before taking from fire add Mazola® and nuts. Pour into tin oiled with Mazola®.

Karo® Caramels

2 cups Granulated Sugar
1 ¾ cups Karo, Blue Label®
½ cup Milk
¼ cup Mazola®
1 teaspoon Vanilla
1 cup Chopped Nuts

Cook sugar, Karo®, milk and Mazola® until it forms a firm ball in cold water. Remove from fire, add vanilla and nuts and pour into pan oiled with Mazola®.

(The three preceding well-used recipes, judging from the wear on the page, were cut out and pasted into the book probably from the label on a Karo® corn syrup bottle.)

Dessert

6 eggs

1 qt. sweet milk

Make boiled custard, beat whites and stir into hot custard. Dissolve ½ **pkg. Knox®** **gelatine** in cold water and stir into custard. Stir in gelatine before whites set. Congeal, slice and serve with **whipped cream.** Flavor with **vanilla.**

Chocolate Nougat Cake

1 cup sugar

½ cup butter

2 eggs

Vanilla

1 cup sour cream

1 teaspoon soda

2 cups flour

2 squares chocolate

1 cup nuts

Cream butter and sugar, add one egg at a time beating thoroughly, add cream with soda beaten into it beforehand. Then add flour, nuts, chocolate, vanilla. Cook slowly.

Oatmeal Raisin Cocoanut Cookies

½ cup lard

¾ cup sugar

1 cup raisins

1 teaspoon baking powder

2 eggs

1 cup flour

1 teaspoon cinnamon

¼ cup sweet milk

½ cup cocoanut

1 cup oatmeal

1/2 teaspoon salt

Tullie's Nut Cake

1 cup butter

2 cups sugar

3 cups flour, 6 eggs

1 nutmeg (if you like) or cinnamon

1 ½ # raisins, 1 quart pecans

1 wineglass whiskey or water

1 teaspoon baking powder

Ginger Cake

1 cup butter

1 cup molasses

1 cup sugar

1 cup buttermilk

4 cups flour

2 tablespoons ginger

2 teaspoons soda

4 eggs

Strawberry Sherbet

1 ¼ cups water

¾ up sugar

1 pint strawberries

1 tablespoon lemon juice

1 egg white

Boil water and sugar five minutes. Cool; add berries, which have been crushed and forced through coarse sieve, and lemon juice. Freeze to a mush. Fold in stiffly beaten egg white and freeze until stiff.

Grape Juice Sherbet

½ envelope Knox Acidulated Gelatine®
½ cup cold water
1 ½ cups boiling water
1 cup sugar
1 pint grape juice
½ cup orange juice

Soak gelatine and ½ teaspoon lemon flavoring, found in separate envelope, in cold water five minutes. Make a syrup by boiling sugar and hot water ten minutes, and add soaked gelatine. Cool slightly and add fruit juice then freeze. Serve in sherbet glasses and garnish with candied violets or fruit, it desired.

Orange Sherbet

(Mine and *Commercial Appeal's*)
1 cup sugar
1/3 cup lemon juice
1 cup orange juice
2 tablespoons grated orange rind
¼ teaspoon salt
2 cups milk or cream

Mix sugar, fruit juices, rind, and salt. Let stand 10 minutes. Slowly add chilled milk. Freeze.

Lemon Apricot Sherbet

(Written in someone else's handwriting, not signed)

Take **one can of apricots**, run through strainer to remove skin. Then add **one cup sugar** and the **grated rind and juice of two lemons**. Then add **1 quart sweet milk** and freeze.

Vanilla Ice Cream

1 cup heavy cream
2/3 cup sugar
1 tablespoon vanilla
1 ½ cups thin cream

Beat the heavy cream until very stiff. Carefully fold into it first the sugar and vanilla, then the thin cream. Freeze.

Chocolate Ice Cream

1 ½ ounces chocolate
2 cups rich milk
1 tablespoon cornstarch
2/3 cup sugar
1 ½ teaspoons vanilla
1 cup heavy cream

Melt chocolate and add scalded milk very slowly. Mix cornstarch with sugar and add to chocolate mixture. Cook ten minutes, stirring constantly until thickened. Cool and add vanilla. Freeze to mush, and then fold in whipped cream and continue freezing until stiff.

Caramel Ice Cream

2 cups rich milk
2 3/4 to 3 cups sugar
Few grains salt
1 tablespoon cornstarch
1 1/2 teaspoons vanilla
1 cup heavy cream

Scald milk. Caramelize sugar in skillet. Add to milk and cook in double boiler until sugar is dissolved. Add salt, and cornstarch mixed with a little milk. Cook ten minutes, stirring constantly until thickened. Cool and add vanilla. Freeze to mush, fold in whipped cream and freeze until stiff.

Pie Pastry

1 ½ cups flour
Mix in ½ teaspoon salt
Scant ½ cup lard

Chop into flour. When lard, salt, and flour are well mixed, add gradually **3 tablespoons water or milk**. Makes 2 crusts.

Orange Pie

1 pint milk
1 egg yolk
2 tablespoons flour
½ cup white sugar
Juice of 2 oranges

Mix the first 3 ingredients thoroughly into the next 2 ingredients. Cook in a steam boiler. When thick, pour it into a **browned crust.** Frost with **meringue made from 2 teaspoons sugar to the white of one egg.**

Sunshine Pie

1 baked crust
4 eggs, separated
4 tablespoons pineapple juice
1 cup sugar, divided
1 tablespoon Knox® gelatine
1 cup crushed pineapple
1 cup nuts

Cook egg yolks, juice, and ½ cup sugar until mixture thickens. Add gelatin dissolved in hot water. Beat 4 egg whites stiff. Add ½ cup sugar, crushed pineapple, and nuts. Mix this with cooked mixture. Put in crust and put in icebox.

Chocolate Pie

1 cup sugar
1 tablespoon cocoa
1 tablespoon flour

Beat 1 egg into this until it takes up sugar and gets smooth. Heat **1 ½ cups milk.** When it begins to boil, stir in mixture, add **teaspoon vanilla** and beat till smooth.

Cocoanut Pie

4 eggs
1 ½ cups sugar
Lump butter
Cocoanut
½ cup sweet milk

Old South Molasses Pie

Boil **two cups of molasses** and **one tablespoon of butter.** Break four eggs in bowl or pan; add **pinch salt,** beat until well mixed. Pour the molasses over the eggs, stirring briskly Have pie pans lined with **crust.** Pour in and bake. This makes two pies. If you wish to make but one pie, equally divide the ingredients.

Old Fashioned Molasses Candy

Put on ¼ **cup butter** in kettle, allow to melt over fire. Then add **two cups molasses**, stir. When well cooked, stir constantly until tried in cold water, candy becomes brittle. Before taking from fire add **1-teaspoon vinegar**. Pour in buttered pan. When cool enough, pull until it becomes light in color. Cut in small pieces with knife of large shears.

Pop Corn Goodies

Boil thoroughly **1 cup molasses** and ½ **cup water**. Add ¼ **cup butter**. Add ½ **teaspoon soda** when candy, tested in cold water, is brittle. Pour over **pop corn** in bowl and stir thoroughly but gently. Roll **pop corn** with slightly buttered hands into balls.

Virginia Peanut Candy

Add 1 cup molasses to ½ cup melted butter. Boil well, then add 1 cupful peanuts (chopped or whole kernels); continue boiling until when tested in cold water, candy is brittle. Pour in buttered pan and cut in small blocks and let cool.

Date Stickies

2 eggs
2/3 cup sugar
3 teaspoons flour before sifting. Sift again
1 teaspoon baking powder
Pinch salt
Few drops vanilla
1 cup chopped dates
1 cup chopped nuts

Spread thin. Bake slowly. Slice.

Shrub

12 lbs. blackberries
5 oz. tartaric acid
2 qts. water
Sugar

Wash berries and put in earthen jar, dissolve tartaric acid in 2 qts. water, pour over berries and let stand 48 hours. Strain and use measure for measure sugar and juice. Stir till sugar dissolved. Bottle but do not seal. Tie cloth over jugs. For strawberries, use 1 ½ measure sugar to each of juice.

Sue Rayner Latham said of this recipe, "I have a feeling that the reason the recipe called for tying it is so it wouldn't explode because I have a feeling it fermented."

Her sister, Cack, added, "It was like blackberry wine, wouldn't you think?" It was legal during Prohibition to make wine at home.

Then Sue said, "Now this is really a sideline. My uncle Wirt Williams who was married to Daddy's sister Nina, taught school at Delta State. He was on the first faculty. He taught history. Now, his mother made blackberry wine, so he had been out to Shrock where his family lived, which is near Goodman, and Uncle Wirt drank some blackberry wine, or brought some home with him, I believe is what it was, and drank some of it, and somebody got wind of it, and I promise he near about lost his job 'cause he was drinking. That's the truth."

Virgie Park Hiter's

Recipe Collection

Virgie Park Hiter's Recipe Collection

Virgie Park was the daughter of Henry and Lucy Rutherford Park. Henry Park arrived in Merigold in 1892 as a store clerk. He needed a place to stay and food to eat, so he decided to operate a boarding house as well. He became partners for a time with J. R. Smith, Sr. who was working as the depot agent in Merigold. Later Mr. Park owned a cotton gin. Virgie was born shortly before the turn of the twentieth century. Merigold Methodist Church records show that she was a student at Buford College in Nashville in 1917. Around 1920 Virgie married Leonard M. Hiter who returned to Merigold from school in Clarksville, Tennessee and joined Merigold Methodist Church in 1917. They had one

son, Henry Hiter, who continued to live on the plantation and continued the farming operation until his retirement.

Leonard Hiter was a planter active in the Merigold community, serving on the school board and the city council, and as a long time Boy Scout leader. He was a charter member of the Merigold Hunting Club. He is pictured at left on a hunt. He was known as a friendly, outgoing man who loved to visit his neighbors and loved to hunt.

Virgie Park Hiter has been characterized as a quiet woman. She stayed close to home and enjoyed raising her family. She helped keep the books for the farm. Virgie and Leonard were active in Merigold Methodist Church, as had been Virgie's parents. The Hammond® organ in Merigold United Methodist Church was given in memory of Lucy Rutherford Park by Virgie Hiter, after the Methodist Women began to try to raise money for the undertaking.

When her grandson, Park Hiter was preparing to move into the old home place built by Leonard and Virgie in Merigold, he discovered a tattered notebook filled with Virgie's handwritten recipes. These are not dated but were likely collected over several years from the 1920s through the 1930s.

Date Loaf

1 pkg. dates
1 tsp. baking soda
1 cup boiling water
2 egg yolks
1 cup sugar
1 T. melted butter
1 cup nuts
2 cups flour
1 teaspoon allspice
1 teaspoon cinnamon

Stone dates.   Put soda over dates and scald with water. Mix egg yolks, sugar, butter, spices, and flour. Add dates and nuts. Pour into greased loaf pan and bake at 350°.

Glorified Peach Individuals

Butter
Brown sugar
Nut meats
Canned or fresh peaches
7/ 8 cup flour
1 tsp. baking powder
1/ 4 tsp. salt
1 cup water
¼ cup water
1 tsp. vanilla
2 eggs, separated, whites beaten

Take muffin tins and grease each with generous dots of butter, sprinkle brown sugar over butter and then over this add a few nutmeats. Add either canned or fresh peaches cut up and over this pour the following batter: Beat yolks of eggs thoroughly. Add sugar and beat well. Add water and dry ingredients alternately. Add vanilla. Lastly, fold in beaten egg whites carefully. Bake in oven 350° for 45 minutes. When done invert on oiled paper and serve with whipped cream.

Chocolate Pie

1 cup sugar
2 teaspoon cocoa
1 tablespoon corn starch, heaped
1 T. butter
Pinch salt
1 tsp. vanilla

Mix sugar, cocoa, and cornstarch. Add butter and salt. Stir constantly until thick over medium heat. Add vanilla. Cool and pour into a baked pie crust. Serve with unsweetened whipped cream.

Chocolate Pie II

Yolks of 4 eggs
1 cup sugar
1 ½ cups milk
½ cup butter
3 or 4 tablespoons cocoa

Heat milk and add cocoa. Then add other ingredients. Cook, stirring constantly, until mixture thickens. Pour into baked pastry crust. Use the egg whites for a meringue topping.

Pastry

1 cup lard
2/3 cup boiling water
3 cups flour
1 teaspoon. salt
1 teaspoon baking powder.

Put lard and boiling water into a bowl. Sift flour, salt and baking powder into a bowl. Mix lard and dry ingredients and stir with spoon till a stiff dough forms. Set away to cool; never use hot. Keep in a cool place. When ready to use, roll out with a pin on a floured surface. Place on pie plate, trim and crimp as desired.

Apple and Rice Custard

Wash **6 tablespoon rice** in several waters and cook. Wash and cut in small pieces **4 small apples.** Cook until soft. Rub apples through sieve and add ½ **cup sugar, 1 well-beaten egg, 1 ½ teaspoon vanilla, and rice**. Bake in a pudding dish.

Lemon Sauce

1 cup sugar
2 ½ tablespoon flour
¼ cup lemon juice
1 tsp. grated lemon rind
¼ cup water

Mix sugar and flour. Add lemon juice, rind and water. Put in saucepan and stir constantly until it reaches boiling point. Put in butter. Stir to prevent sticking to pan.

Molasses Cake

1 heaped teaspoon butter
1 ½ cups sugar
3 eggs
1 cup sour milk
2 teaspoons soda, wet with a little hot water
1 cup molasses
1 tablespoon cinnamon
1 teaspoon cloves
Pinch ginger
3 cups flour
Pinch salt

Mix all ingredients and pour into a greased cake pan (s) and bake in medium oven until done.

Harrison Cake

¾ cup butter
¾ cup sugar
½ cup dark molasses mixed with ¼ tsp. soda
¼ cup milk
½ teaspoon cinnamon
½ teaspoon cloves
½ teaspoon salt
3 eggs
1 cup chopped raisins
2 ½ cups flour
3 teaspoons baking powder

Cream butter thoroughly. Add sugar and mix in molasses. Sift flour, salt, spices, and baking powder together and add half, beating well. Add milk and well-beaten egg yolks. Add rest of dry ingredients and raisins dredged in flour. Lastly, add beaten egg whites. Bake in a loaf in moderate oven 1 hour. To prevent raisins from sinking in cake, heat them before rolling in flour.

Spice Cake

4 eggs
1 ½ cups sugar
½ cup butter
1 cup buttermilk
1 teaspoon soda
2 cups flour
2 tablespoons molasses
1 tablespoon cinnamon
1 tablespoon cloves
1 tablespoon allspice
1 tablespoon nutmeg
Raisins and nuts may be added if desired.

Mix all ingredients.   Pour into pan(s) and bake at 350 degrees until done.

Mrs. Ming's Black Chocolate Cake

Chocolate sauce for cake batter:
½ cake chocolate
1 cup sugar
½ cup sweet milk
1 egg
1 teaspoon vanilla

Mix, cook until thick.   Let cool before using in cake.

½ cup butter
1 cup sugar
3 eggs, separated and well-beaten
2 cups flour
2 teaspoon baking powder
½ cup sweet milk

Cream butter and sugar. Add yolks. Add chocolate mixture from above. Fold in well beaten egg whites last. Bake at 350 degrees until done.

Icing for above
1 cake chocolate
½ cup butter
1 cup hot water
2 cups sugar

Cook till crisp. Beat till cool and ice quickly.

Chocolate Layer Cake

½ cup butter

1 ½ cups sugar

3 cups cake flour

3 teaspoons baking powder

¼ teaspoon salt

½ cup milk

½ cup water

1-teaspoon vanilla

¼ teaspoon. almond flavoring

3 egg whites, beaten light

Cream shortening; add sugar. Sift flour and measure. Then sift together flour, baking powder, and salt. Beat into first mixture alternately with water and mil. Beat in flavoring. Fold in egg whites.

Chocolate Frosting:

Cut 4 squares bitter chocolate into small pieces into pan. Add 1 cup sugar and 1 ½ cups milk. Bring to boil stirring. Mix 3 tablespoons cornstarch and 2 tablespoons cold water. Add slowly to first mixture. Stir till thick. Remove; add 2 tablespoons butter and flavoring.

Fruit Cake

1 lb. butter

1 lb. sugar (2 cups)

1 lb. flour (3 cups)

7 eggs

1 ½ lb. raisins (2 packages)

1 lb. dried currants

¾ lb. dried citron

1 pint shelled pecans

1 cup molasses

1 cup blackberry jam

½ nutmeg grated

1 pint figs

1 teaspoon each cloves, all-spice, cinnamon, mace, and ginger

1 full teaspoon baking powder

Add candied cherries as desired

Mix all ingredients and bake from 3 to 4 hours in a slow oven. After 20 or 30 minutes, put pan of water in oven. Yields 8 lbs. fruitcake.

Birthday Cake

1 ½ cups sugar

¾ cups butter

4 eggs

¾ cup milk

3 cups flour with 3 T. baking powder

¼ tsp. salt

2 T. orange juice

1-teaspoon vanilla

Cream butter and sugar. Mix in eggs, milk, and dry ingredients. Pour into greased and floured layer pans and bake in a medium oven until done. Fill with fruit filling as described below:

Pineapple or Banana Filling:

Put 1 cup milk on to boil. Mix 1 tablespoon cornstarch with a little water and add to milk. Let boil 3 minutes stirring. Beat 3 eggs without separating and 1 tablespoon sugar until light and add to boiling milk. Stir well to keep from burning. Put layer of fruit (pineapple or bananas) over cake and sprinkle with powdered sugar, then spread with filling. Ice or sprinkle top with powdered sugar on top.

White Cake

Whites of 5 eggs, beaten stiff

1 cup butter

2 cups sugar

3 cups flour

2 rounded, not heaping teaspoons baking powder

Pinch of salt

¾ cup milk

Cream butter and sugar. Sift together flour, baking powder, and salt. Combine with the creamed mixture and stir in milk. Fold in stiff egg whites. Divine into layer pans and bake in a medium oven until done.

Oatmeal Cookies

1 ½ cups sugar

1 cup butter

2 cups oatmeal

2 ¼ cups flour

2 eggs, beaten separately

1 heaping teaspoon cinnamon

1 level teaspoon soda, dissolved in 4 tablespoons sweet milk

2 cups raisins

1-cup nuts

Cream butter and sugar. Add oatmeal, flour, eggs, soda, milk, and cinnamon. Mix well, and then add the raisins and nuts. Drop on greased cookie tin and bake in a medium oven.

Golden Custard with Meringue

6 eggs, separated

6 tablespoons sugar

1 teaspoon melted butter

1-½ tablespoons flour

1 quart sweet milk, heated to boiling point

To egg yolks add sugar, butter and flour. Beat until smooth. Heat the milk and beat into above mixture and cook until it begins to thicken. Beat the egg whites. Add **6 table-spoons sugar and vanilla** to taste. Drop whites on custard and brown in oven.

Rice Pudding

½ cup rice

4 apples, peeled, cored, and stewed

1 ½ pints milk

1/3 cup sugar

4 eggs, separated

Cook rice. Add applesauce, egg yolks, and sugar. Let cool. Mix in stiffly beaten egg whites. Pour into dish and set in pan of boiling water for 55 minutes.

Marshmallow Pudding

Soak **1 T. gelatine in ½ cup cold water**. Add **1/2 cup hot water**. As it cools, add **2 stiffly beaten egg whites with 2/3 cup sugar**. When half congealed, alternate layers with **pineapple, citron, raisins, cherries, and nuts**. Serve with **whipped cream**.

Apple Float

1 dozen apples
Nutmeg
Sugar
Egg whites

Cook apple till tender, beat until smooth and sweeten to taste. When cold, add one egg white well beaten to every 1 cup of apples. Flavor and serve with boiled custard or cream.

Food Memories
from the
Merigold Hunting Club

Merigold Hunting Club

The Merigold Hunting and Fishing Club is considered the "Father of the Mississippi Delta hunting clubs." It was loosely organized several years prior to its official chartering in 1921.

According to the recollections of Mari Ana Pemble Davis, the original caretaker was Uncle Jack, who was quiet and reserved. The next ones were Pat and Polly. Pat was the wife and she was from Idaho. Polly was a local "River Rat" and knew all about what was needed for survival on the river. His job included making sure the fishing boats were emptied after a rain. "He and Pat once drove back to Idaho to visit her family in an old Model A Ford—and they made it!" Mrs. Davis said.

The best-known cook was William Franklin, a Black cook who could work magic with game and fish. He would cook in big pots over a fire and prepare whatever had been killed—deer, squirrel, wild turkey—or just fry fish. He would fix big pots of vegetables—whatever was in season and always lots of potatoes. Mari Ana Davis remembers, "He and his helpers always wore white aprons and looked real nice" (until the realities of cooking took their toll).

Wives would come out at noon during a hunt to eat lunch and also many came for supper there. Originally the club just had a dining hall where everyone ate. It is still there. Later, some of the owners built cabins. The Ed Pembles and the Leonard Hiters built a duplex cabin and shared a screened porch. Before the cabins, the men would all just sleep in the one big room together. If someone snored, the rest just had to deal with it, Davis said.

Pat Wynne now lives full time at the Merigold Hunting Club. He said that years ago, none of the cooks had figured out how to successfully cook venison. He said, "They'd fix it, but it was like shoe leather." Through years of experimentation, they finally developed a method to make it tender and delicious every time.

In an interview with Carrie Huff (pictured above on the right), who is today's chief cook during the fall hunts, she recounted her history of cooking at the club. She said she has been working there for the past twenty-two years. She grew up in Lobdell, just two or three miles from the club. She was living on the Jimmy House plantation there and he asked her if she would be interested in working at the hunting club. She worked first as a dishwasher, when the head cook was a man named Norman. Others who worked there when she started were Lucy Winfrey, Eddie Vaughn, Bernice King and William whom she called "Pops." She said she learned how to cook venison from Norman and then added her own touches through the years. This is the way she prepares the venison that is provided by the hunters daily during the fall hunts:

> The skinners dress the deer and hang it in a walk-in refrigerator to chill for at least a half a day. You just can't cut it when it is still warm. It has to be good and cold, then they cut it up into small pieces. When I get it, I soak it in water with a little salt in it to loosen any hair that might still be on it. After I wash it good, I put it through the tenderizing machine. That's one thing I changed from the way they used to do it. Norman would just put it through once or twice.

And before they got the tenderizing machine, they had to use a mallet, so they didn't get it as tender as I do. Now I do it at least five or six times. After that, you can just put your fingers through it, it is so tender. Then I take each piece and sprinkle all sides with Lawry's Seasoned Salt®, then with black pepper, onion powder, and meat tenderizer. Then I marinate it in Worcestershire sauce. I let it stay in that for at least thirty minutes, but it can stay in it up to three days in the refrigerator before it is cooked.

When I am ready to cook the meat, I put more of the Lawry's®, pepper, and onion powder into some flour. Then I coat the meat in the seasoned flour. I fry it in a great big iron skillet filled about half full with Wesson® oil. I test the oil by dropping a little flour in it. When I drop it in and it sizzles, I know it's right. Then I fry each piece just three to five minutes, turning only once or twice. It cooks real fast, because it is already so tender, and the Worcestershire sauce has already almost cooked it. I serve this at every lunch and supper during the hunts, along with whatever else I serve.

Venison is not the only thing Carrie Huff cooks at the hunting club meals. As a matter of fact, she cooks a veritable feast every day of the two hunts. The club has a big hunt every year beginning the Friday before Thanksgiving and continuing until the Sunday after Thanksgiving. They have another one beginning on the evening Christmas Day and concluding the Sunday after New Year's Day. During these two hunts, she prepares three meals a day, along with her staff, Joseph Taylor, Shirley Banks, Mecci Lewis, and Carrie's daughter Tawanda Huff. On holidays, Linda Taylor also helps out.

For breakfast, they serve on average about twenty-five to thirty diners. They offer bacon, eggs, sausage, grits, biscuits, toast, orange juice, milk and coffee and serve from 5:30 to 8:00 a.m. For lunch and dinner, they serve an average of fifty to seventy-five diners at each meal. Lunch is served from 11:30 to 1:30 and dinner is served from 5:30 to 7:30. Huff says they typically have several side dishes along with main dishes like fried chicken, fried fish, or spaghetti. Of course, there is always the fried venison.

The only time she doesn't serve venison is for the special holiday meals. On these days, they feed one hundred fifty to two hundred, since the hunters bring in their extended families. For the holiday meals, she cooks traditional holiday fare such as turkey and dressing with all the trimmings.

Below are three recipes from the hunters at the club. One is from the 1950s when an essential tools in every cook's kitchen was a pressure cooker. The others are favorites of today's cooks.

Venison Steaks

(from the 1950s church cookbook)

First, ask your hunter to bag a Spike Buck the first day of the November Hunt when deer are still fat. If he should bring home a 12-point beauty in December, don't be discouraged. (Hang either kind in a walk-in refrigerator at a locker for 2 weeks before butchering.)

Thaw tough or wild tasting steaks in cool water to which ½ cup vinegar has been added. The young, tender buck meat will not need this step. Drain. Salt and pepper very generously (the pepper is especially important). Cover with flour, brown in a pressure cooker. Add the following:

2 large onions, sliced

1 large bell pepper, chopped

Water as called for by your pressure cooker

(I use 1 ½ cups water so my gravy is made when cooking time is up)

Cover and cook 20 minutes after steam has reached "Cook" on your pressure cooker (30 minutes for tougher steaks).

Serve with plenty of rice and gravy made from stock in pressure cooker.

Gene Wynne

Gene was the wife of Frank Wynne, Jr. who was an avid second-generation member of the Merigold Hunting Club. He joined after he returned home from serving in World War II, where he spent 30 months as a prisoner of war in Japan. He credited many of the lessons he learned in Boy Scouts at Merigold for equipping him to endure and survive the difficulties of captivity. In civilian life, Mr. Wynne practiced law and traveled all over the world as a hunter and sportsman. Mrs. Wynne was a schoolteacher at Merigold, and a wife who learned how to cook and serve some of her husband's bounty from beyond the levee.

Jim's Grilled Doves

Doves, dressed and de-boned

Wishbone Italian dressing

Bacon

Marinate doves in dressing overnight. Wrap each dove in a small piece of bacon. Secure with a toothpick. Grill for a few minutes on each side, using a fish basket.

Jim Meyer

A variation on this recipe adds a jalapeno pepper and a bit of cream cheese to the doves before wrapping in the bacon.

Fried Wild Turkey Breast Strips

Wild turkey breast

Milk

Flour

Seasonings as desired

Slice turkey breast into small strips. Soak in milk. Mix flour and seasonings together. Dredge in flour and fry in oil until golden brown.

Jim Meyer

Jim Meyer is a grandson of Ed Rayner and maintains a cabin at Merigold Hunting Club today. The Meyers join together for a Christmas Day celebration at the cabin each year for loads of food and presents.

Rev. Billy Owen performed the first wedding ceremony to be held at Merigold United Methodist Church in over ten years, on August 9, 2003, when Jim and Mitsi Meyer were married in a beautifully decorated setting. In the tradition of Jim's grandmother, Bess Rayner, a sumptuous reception dinner was held at the home of the groom's parents, Johnny and Cack Meyer, following the wedding.

The Cooks of the 1950s

Food Trends of the 1940s and 1950s

The rationing enforced during World War II changed the way people cooked and ate radically. Wartime cooking revolved around protein stretching, substitutions, sugarless cookies, eggless cakes, and meatless meals. From 1942 through 1945 sugar, coffee, processed foods, meats, canned fish, cheese, canned milk, and fats were rationed, so that the available supply was distributed evenly to the whole population. With the American government's huge promotion of Victory Gardens, people went back to the way their mothers and grandmothers had cooked, only without some common staple items. Rationing stamps were carefully used. Sugar was reserved for special occasions such as birthday celebrations or homecomings. Some said that by the end of the war, people had just about forgotten how to cook, because they had been forced to "make do" for so long.

Food was not the only thing rationed. All things having to do with transportation were also rationed. Tires, cars, gasoline—even bicycles—were rationed. A family-car that was deemed for "nonessential" purposes (those not owned by defense workers, physicians, ministers, mail carriers, or railroad workers) was limited to four gallons of gasoline per week. Cack Meyer and Sue Latham remembered with a chuckle the time a gas tanker truck overturned in downtown Merigold during the war. They said everybody in town went running to the site of the accident carrying pails, bowls, buckets, virtually anything they could find that would hold gas. As the tanker spilled its valuable cargo, their mother sent them running with milk churns. The ration-weary people of Merigold didn't allow a drop to waste. During the war, the "victory speed limit" was thirty-five miles per hour, to save both gasoline and tires for the war effort. It was considered an insult to one's neighbors for anyone to go to Cleveland or Clarksdale with an empty seat in a car. Carpooling was the order of the time, and the Southerner's love of story telling was practiced and enjoyed on the shared trips.

By the time the war ended, more women than ever before were in the work force outside the home. Research done by the military during the war resulted in the postwar introduction of many new convenience foods such as instant coffee and tea, cake mixes, pie crust mixes, and Minute Rice®. Although these foods were available, they were typically slow to catch on in Merigold, because most preferred to serve meals the old fashioned way. Merigold Methodist Church did not have "potluck" meals, but occasionally had "appreciation dinners" for groups in the community such as educators.

The most noticeable change in food trends during the 1950s was the emergence of the casserole. Although they have been around for centuries in some form or another as one pot meals, the quick, filling, and inexpensive varieties of casseroles that cooks dreamed up continued to expand exponentially through at least the 1970s. Ubiquitous in the 1950s was the tuna casserole, made with readily available ingredients such as canned tuna, packaged noodles, canned creamed soups and evaporated milk. It was sometimes topped with buttered bread or cracker crumbs and browned in the oven.

Other popular foods of the fifties included tuna salad, three bean salad, Chex® mix, and Tang® (introduced in 1958). Commonly served at ladies' gatherings were deviled eggs and celery hearts stuffed with Cheeze Whiz® (introduced in 1953). A favorite dip for potato chips was made with sour cream and a new product introduced in 1952 called Lipton Onion Soup Mix®. Coco Cola's Mississippi Delta arch rival, Royal Crown (RC) Cola® was launched in 1959. Today in Merigold and in nearby Cleveland and Delta State University, RC products are very popular due to the local community support given to the region by the Sledges, owners of the local Nehi Bottling Company since the 1920s.

Not long after most homes in Merigold had electricity, the home freezer changed the way food was preserved. Becoming popular in the 1940s, these food freezers grew more common in homes throughout the 1950s and beyond. It became common to buy frozen vegetables at the grocery stores. Post war cooks were also introduced to frozen French fries and fish sticks. No longer did fresh vegetables picked in gardens have the be canned in glass jars under pressure. Now the produce could be blanched and put in square plastic boxes or in plastic bags and kept in the home freezer. Pork was now available at times other than in the cold weather "hog-killing" season. Meat that used to require smoking, salting, or canning, could now be frozen. Later, frost-free home freezers were introduced, eliminating the back breaking chore of defrosting that would typically take a whole day.

The women of Merigold continued their tradition of serving hearty meals to their families. Women's church societies flourished during this time and functioned as the most important social event of the weekday. They usually featured beautifully presented finger sandwiches, desserts, punch or soft drinks, nuts, and mints. Most tables were spread with starched linens, china, and silver, even on a summer afternoon. The women's groups expanded their cooking to include annual fundraisers for mission and church projects. It would not be until several decades later that church potlucks would become common.

A Brief History of the Merigold WSCS

I was told by Mrs. J. A. (Shirley) Westerfield, that in the early days of Merigold, there was a white frame building on the lot where the park is today. The denominations that had a congregation shared the building on Sundays and it was used as a school on weekdays. Among the most important groups to the community were its women's church societies, with each denomination having its own group. In 1896, the Methodist

church built its own frame structure (pictured above) on the lot where the present day church is. The Methodist church had a women's society for many years, as evidenced by the stained glass window placed in the 1920 church building still in use today. In 1939 there was a Uniting Conference in Kansas City, Missouri that united Methodists worldwide. Following this, the Women's Society of Christian Service was chartered in 1940 and the women of Merigold Methodist Church followed suit. At their local chartering meeting on September 9, 1940 there were thirty-three women present. The WSCS met monthly on Monday afternoons at 3:00 in the homes of various members, with other members assisting them as hostesses. The one who hosted each month's meeting was also responsible for seeing that flowers were in the church each Sunday of her month.

A great honor for a member of the WSCS was to be made a lifetimemember, through the group's vote and donation to the national organization. The lifetime members of the Merigold WSCS as of 1956 are painstakingly written on a black scrapbook page in white ink by the official scrapbook keeper, Ethlyn Fincher Speakes. The thirty-three lifetime members included Mrs. W. M Beck, Mrs. W. H. Bernard, Mrs. A. B. Booth, Sr., Mrs. A. B. Booth, Jr., Mrs. George Cox, Mrs. C. R. Gramling, Mrs. R. E. Gramling, Mrs. R. A. Hall, Mrs. E. B. Hill, Mrs. L. M. Hiter, Mrs. W. O Hunt, Mrs. F. E. Jones, Mrs. C. D. Kitching, Mrs. Alice Latham, Mrs. Charles Lawrence, Mrs. C. F. Kittle, Mrs. A. L. Moreland, Mrs. Charles Moreland, Mrs. J. P. McLaurin, Miss Ida Newby, Mrs. L. A. Peeples, Mrs. H. E. Ramsey, Mrs. E. D. Rayner, Mrs. G. C. Richardson, Mrs. Paul Robertson, Mrs. A. J. Smith, Mrs. Ernest Smith, Mrs. H. E. Speakes, Mrs. T. H. Thornton, Mrs. J. A. Westerfield, Mrs. A. M. Wynne, Mrs. Harry Wiltshire, and Mrs. M. C. Waldrop.

At each meeting, the programs included a lesson about issues and needs from around the globe, so this organization helped the women have a larger perspective than just of Merigold or Mississippi, or even the USA. They frequently had extended studies on countries such as Bolivia and Korea. In addition to a devotional, the business, and a formal mission study, the women usually sang one or two hymns and heard a poem recited. Following a closing prayer, they would enjoy refreshments prepared with great care and served on silver trays by the hostesses on tables decked with fresh flowers from their yards.

The churches in Merigold did not often have potluck dinners during these years, but the women of the WSCS were still busy cooking for the community. Clippings from the WSCS scrapbook mention the plans to give a potluck supper in honor of the faculty members at Merigold School. More frequently, the WSCS worked together to cook meals as fundraisers for missions or to purchase needed items for the church or the parsonage. They often cooked meals for the meetings of the North Delta Shrine Club and for the Merigold Hunting and Fishing Club as well.

In the late 1930s and 40s, the WSCS took on the task of providing the meal for the weekly Wednesday noon meetings of the Exchange Club of Merigold. Bess Rayner planned the meals and divided the duties among the members. A typical meal would be Chicken Pie with two or three in-season garden vegetables, a dessert, and beverage. Other weeks' main dishes might be fried chicken, turkey and dressing, or baked ham. The duties alternated so that one week a member would provide a vegetable and another week she would contribute $1.00 toward purchasing the meat. Mrs. Sara Davis always cooked the cornbread, and Mrs. Wynne's maid, Arie, always cooked the rice. These meetings were held at the American Legion Hut in Merigold, which had a full kitchen for their use, located where the public library is today.

The United Methodist Women fed the Methodist Men's Club once a month. Every woman was asked to contribute to the meal. If she did not could not cook or provide food, she was asked to donate one dollar toward the cost of the meat. Fresh vegetables from their gardens or freezers were in great supply. Whatever foods were in season were part of the menu. Mrs. Jeanette Hill always prepared the homemade rolls. They were delivered hot from her kitchen. Some 160 rolls were devoured in no time.

Each spring in the 1950s and 60s, Cack Meyer says, "When the jonquils were in bloom, the Merigold Methodist Women cooked for their annual Spaghetti Day. As many as 200 were served for lunch in the fellowship hall. Tickets were $3.00 a plate. Every lady contributed toward the meal. We served Spaghetti Meat Sauce over pasta with a green salad, French bread or rolls, and cake squares for dessert." These Spaghetti Days provided much of the funding for many projects such as buying bibles for prisoners at nearby Parchman Penitentiary, or supporting an orphan to go to college, or many other worthwhile needs.

The roll recipe they used was from Mrs. E. B. (Jeanette) Hill who always supervised the roll making.

Mrs. Jeanette Hill's Rolls

1cup milk
½ cup sugar
½ cup shortening (margarine can be used)
3 cups flour
½ teaspoon soda
½ teaspoon baking powder
2 teaspoons salt
1 pkg. yeast

Scald milk; add to sugar and shortening. When lukewarm, add 1 package yeast dissolved in a little lukewarm water. To this mixture, add enough flour to make soft dough. Set aside in warm place for about 2 hours or until double in bulk. Sift balance of flour with 1/2 teaspoon each of soda and baking powder, and 2 teaspoons salt. Add to first mixture, mixing well. Roll out and cut with a biscuit cutter. Let rise about 2 hours. Bake at 400° for 15 minutes. Makes about 60 rolls. This can be doubled to make about 120 rolls.

Mrs. Jeanette Hill was the wife of Edward Bibb Hill. She was the widow of Mr. Atlee B. Wiggins who had been a partner in the Smith and Wiggins plantation and cotton ginning operation. He was also a county supervisor. He died in 1932 during his term of office and Ed Rayner was selected to finish his term and was then elected to serve another full term. Mr. and Mrs. Wiggins experienced a terrible tragedy on Christmas Day when their eleven-year-old son died during a routine surgery. There is a stained glass window in the son's memory at Merigold United Methodist Church. Mrs. Wiggins later married Mr. Hill of Cleveland. She was a very active member of the Methodist church in Merigold and was a leader in organizing many activities.

Below is the recipe they used for their Spaghetti Day meat sauce.

Spaghetti Meat Sauce

1 lb. ground meat
1 lb. can crushed tomatoes
8-oz. tomato paste
1 tablespoon chili powder
1 teaspoon sugar
1 teaspoon salt
1 teaspoon black pepper
1 bay leaf
1 large green pepper, chopped
1 large onion, chopped
1 ribs celery chopped

Brown meat. Add onion after meat loses its pink color. Add celery. Cook until celery is limp. Add tomatoes, tomato paste, and all seasonings. Cook and stir often for about 1-½ hours or until all vegetables are cooked. Add bell pepper and cook until pepper is limp.
[I triple my recipe and package it for the freezer. It is always ready to thaw and reheat for "drop-ins."]

Cack Meyer

It was during the mid 1950s that the women of Merigold Methodist Church got together and invited their friends and neighbors to contribute recipes to their church cookbook. This cookbook is presented here in its entirety, along with excerpts from local news stories from the society columns about their meetings and special events.

The 1950s Cookbook
of the
Merigold Methodist Church's
Woman's Society of Christian Service

MERIGOLD'S
FAVORITE RECIPES

Compiled by
The Woman's Society of Christian Service
MERIGOLD METHODIST CHURCH

The Merigold Methodist Church Woman's Society of Christian Service Cookbook of the 1950s listed the following:

Pastor—Rev. J. G. Babb
President—Mrs. Robert Gramling
VP—Mrs. George Cox
Secretary—Mrs. G. C. Richardson
Treasurer—Mrs. E. B. Hill

Members:
Mrs. J. G. Babb
Mrs. W. M Beck
Mrs. W. H. Bernard
Mrs. Albert Booth, Jr.
Mrs. Albert Booth, Sr.

Mrs. C. R. Gramling
Mrs. F. E. Jones
Mrs. Robert Hall
Mrs. L. M Hiter
Mrs. O. D. Kitching
Mrs. Alice Latham
Mrs. Charles Lawrence
Mrs. J. P. McLaurin
Mrs. A. L. Moreland
Miss Ida Newby
Mrs. L. A. Peeples
Mrs. H. E. Ramsey
Mrs. E. D. Rayner
Mrs. L. P. Robertson
Mrs. Ernest Smith
Mrs. Margaret A. Smith
Mrs. Harry Speakes
Mrs. T. H. Thornton
Mrs. A. M . Wynne
Mrs. J. A. Westerfield

Recipes from the 1950s Cookbook

Dill Pickles

>1 gallon water
>¾ cup salt
>½ cup white vinegar

Boil these 3 ingredients together. Wash cucumbers or small green tomatoes of uniform size. Place in sterilized quart jars. Pour above hot mixture over cucumbers or tomatoes and just before sealing, put in

>1 T. pickling spice
>a couple of garlic buttons, (cut through)
>dill (fresh is much better that prepared dill)

Seal while hot and for several days, a cloudy residue will form at the bottom of the jar. Run upside down every day so this will penetrate the pickles. Takes about 3 weeks to "make," then they are ready.

>Mrs. A. M. Wynne

Chow Chow

>1 peck green tomatoes
>1 T. salt
>6 large onions
>4 cups sugar
>1- 10 cent box mixed spices
>2 medium sized cabbages
>6 red bell peppers or 3 hot peppers
>2 qt. Vinegar

Put tomatoes, cabbages, onions, and pepper through food chopper. Drain all the juice out of it and put in large kettle. Add salt, sugar and cover with vinegar. Tie spices in thin cloth and drop in mixture. Cook for 20 to 30 minutes after it comes to a boil. Seal.

>Mrs. Bertha Smith

Mrs. Polly Lamb's Sweet Tomato Pickles

>2 gallons water
>3 cups lime
>7 lbs. green tomatoes, sliced
>2 lbs. raisins
>4 ½ lbs. Sugar
>3 qts. vinegar

Cinnamon, cloves, celery seed and allspice to suit taste, placed in a spice bag

Mix lime in water. Add tomatoes. Let stand 24 hours. Rinse in clear cold water; let stand in cold water 2 hours. Boil sugar, vinegar and spices 5 minutes. Drain tomatoes and pour vinegar mixture over them. Let stand 24 hours, add raisins and boil 15 minutes. Seal in hot jars.

Mrs. Parker West

Piccalilli

First, wash **1 peck (8 quarts) of green tomatoes,** then cut out their stem ends and quarter them. Next, wash

> 12 red sweet peppers
> 12 green peppers

Cut each pepper in half; remove the seeds and fibrous portions; quarter them. Last, peel and quarter **1 quart of small onions.** With the tomatoes, peppers and onions prepared, set up your food chopper and grind the vegetables. Drain off the liquid and discard it. Turn the drained vegetables into a large kettle; add **2 quarts cider vinegar** and boil, uncovered, 20 minutes, stirring frequently with a long-handled spoon. Again drain vegetables, discarding liquid, then with the drained vegetables back in the large kettle, stir in the following ingredients:

> 1-quart cider vinegar
> 7 cups sugar
> ½ cup salt
> 1 cup mustard seed
> 3-tablespoons celery seed
> 1-tablespoon cinnamon
> 1 tablespoon powdered allspice

Simmer the mixture, uncovered, for 3 minutes. Now, pack the piccalilli immediately into sterilized jars. This will make 12 pints.

Clara Robertson

Cucumber Pickle

1 gallon large cucumbers, sliced

Add **3 cups household lime** to **2 gallons of water.** Pour this over cucumbers and let it stand for 24 hours. Soak cucumbers in 4 different clear waters for 1 hour in each water. Make a syrup of **3 lbs. of sugar to 1 quart vinegar and 6 T. mixed spices.** Pour this over cucumbers and let this stand overnight. Next morning, cook for 1 hour and seal.

Mrs. G. C. Richardson

Virginia Chunk Sweet Pickles

75 cucumbers, 4 or 5 inches long, or 2 gallons small ones
(Or use what you have, most any nice solid cucumbers make nice pickles.) Make brine of a proportion of **2 cups of salt to 1 gallon water**. Boil and pour over cucumbers while boiling hot. Let stand 1 week. In hot weather, skim daily. Drain and cut in chunks. For the next 3 mornings, make a boiling hot solution of **1 gallon water and 1 T. powdered alum**. Pour over the pickles. Make this fresh hot bath for three mornings. On the 4th morning, drain from alum water. Heat together

> 6 cups vinegar
> 5 cups sugar
> 1/3 cup pickling spice
> 1 T. celery seed

Bring to boiling point and pour over pickles. Fifth morning, drain this liquid off, add **2 cups more of sugar**; heat and pour over pickles. Sixth morning, drain liquid; add **1 cup sugar**; heat. Pack pickles in sterilized jars and pour this liquid over until the jar is filled. Seal at once.

Mrs. E. B. Hill

Nippy Cheese Dip

1 3 oz. Pkg. Cream cheese
3 oz. Bleu cheese
2 T. cream
1 T. minced onion
2 T. chopped ripe olives

Mash cream cheese with fork. Add crumbled Bleu cheese and cream to make of spreading consistency. Add onion and chopped olives. Blend thoroughly. Pile lightly in dish and serve with assorted crackers or potato chips.

Mrs. Bobby McArthur

Vegetable Soup

3 quarts water
1 soup bone
1 pkg. Frozen mixed vegetables
1 10-oz. Can tomatoes
1 medium sized potato
1 medium sized onion
Salt and pepper to taste

Start water and soup bone over slow fire. When soup bone is done, add frozen vegetables. Thirty minutes later, add tomatoes. Thirty minutes before serving time, add chopped potato and chopped onion. Cooking time should be about 1½ hours.

Mrs. James A. Westerfield

This is Shirley Wynne Westerfield, daughter of Dr. A. M. Wynne and wife of the physician who later joined him in practice in Merigold. Dr. Westerfield "was a gregarious type of man who loved people—loved to be with people," said Cack Meyer. Dr. Westerfield graduated near the top of his class at University of Tennessee Medical School. He had to leave during World War II and served in the Aleutians. He and Shirley married during those years, and many believe that Shirley was the reason Merigold was able to keep such a fine physician. Their son Andrew Westerfield is the mayor of Merigold today.

Dr. Tony Scarborough recalled this experience with Dr. Westerfield:

"We bought our Merigold house in 1978 and I spent about two years working on it before making it just barely habitable, and close to ten years to finish it. The elderly Dr. Westerfield lived two doors down the street from us, and every morning he came walking past our house on his way to the little brick building downtown that he called his office. We would greet and speak frequently. Dr. Westerfield was a country doctor from the old school. That put him as a traveling doctor making house calls with his black bag in the Mississippi Delta during the Great Depression years.

"I had lots of construction and destruction going on at the same time. There were frequently boards, bricks, and junk lying about to be tip-toed over. One day I was outdoors carrying a big arm load of lumber so that I couldn't very well see where I was stepping. I stepped onto a board that had a large nail sticking through it. I can remember the event as if in slow motion, my right foot in an old tennis shoe pressing down upon the point of the nail, the pressure building, followed by a sharp "pop" as the nail punctured the sole of my shoe. An instant later, the nail was protruding from the top of my foot.

"I dropped the load I was carrying and shook off the board, which was firmly nailed into my foot. The nail looked clean: it was a new one. Consequently, I wasn't worried much about tetanus or some other infection. Nevertheless, I sat down on the steps, took my shoe off, and massaged that foot for quite a while, then put the shoe back on and went to work again. A couple of days later, the foot began to turn pink and swell. I went to Dr. Westerfield's downtown office for medical attention. The office shelves were lined with what seemed to be medical antiques, although he surely still used them

as needed. I took off my right shoe and told him what had happened as he examined my swollen foot. He decided that I did indeed need a tetanus shot. He told his nurse to go to his house, go to the kitchen, and look in the refrigerator door and bring him the vaccine! A little while later she returned with a chilled vial of tetanus vaccine. He administered the shot. I asked him how much his charges were. He thought for a moment and tentatively said, 'Five dollars,' then added apologetically, 'That vaccine is expensive.' The office visit was $2, the vaccine, $3. I thanked him, paid up, and went on my way. The office visit was worth much more than $5 just for the smiles I got from the experience."

Dr. Tony Scarborough

Oyster Stew

In a large saucepan, combine
2 tablespoon flour
1 1/2 teaspoons salt
¼ teaspoon pepper
2 tablespoons water

Blend these ingredients together to a smooth paste. Add **1 pint oysters and their liquor**. Simmer mixture over low heat until oysters' edges curl. Carefully pour in **1 quart scalded milk**. Remove pan from heat; cover and let stand 15 minutes. This improves the flavor. Just before serving, add **1/2 stick of butter** (1/4 cup). Reheat soup until it is piping hot. Have soup tureen and soup plates hot. With oyster crackers and a dish of crisp relishes, this rich soup is a meal in itself.

Mrs. Robert Gramling

Frosty Fruit Salad

1 3-oz. package cream cheese
1-cup mayonnaise
1-cup heavy cream, whipped
1 # 2 ½ can fruit cocktail, drained
½ cup drained maraschino cherries (quartered)
1-½ cups (about 24) diced marshmallows

Soften cream cheese and blend with mayonnaise. Fold in remaining ingredients. Add a few drops red food coloring or cherry juice to tint light pink, if desired. To freeze, pour into 2 one quart round ice cream or freezer containers. Freeze firm, about 6 hours or overnight. To serve, slice in rounds and place on crisp lettuce. Do not store in freezer more than two months.

Mrs. L. A. Peeples

Norman's Salad Bowl

2 peeled tomatoes, cut in wedges
½ cup finely shredded cucumber
½ cup radishes, chopped
1 head lettuce
1 cup diced celery
1 small onion, finely chopped
1/3 cup chopped pecans
½ cup Kraft's French dressing
Salt and pepper to taste

Place all vegetables and pecans in salad bowl. Pour over dressing and toss lightly. Makes 6 servings.

Norman Kealhofer
[He was the brother of Mrs. J. S. Fincher]

Snowballs

12 big canned Alberta peach halves, drained
Fill cavities with this mixture:
3 oz. pkg. cream cheese, softened
Sweet cream
1/3 cup chopped pecan meats

Place filled peach halves together to form whole peaches on **endive or lettuce**. Top with meringue made as follows: Beat **2 egg whites** until frothy, add **4 T. sugar** and beat until glossy and firm but not dry, and fold **1 T. mayonnaise**. Spread meringue over peaches to resemble snowballs.

Olyve Wynne

Olyve Wynne was the wife of Dr. Wynne and the mother of Shirley Westerfield and Nell Wynne. She was the former Olyve O'Brien of Appleton, Wisconsin. She was a very proper, formal lady who made afternoon calls in her gloves and hat. She taught a Sunday school class at the Methodist church.

Tomato Soup Salad

3 pkgs. cream cheese

1 can tomato soup

1 envelope gelatin, dissolved in 1 cup cold water

1 cup chopped celery

1 cup nuts

1 cup mayonnaise

1 small green pepper

Salt to taste

Heat soup and cream cheese in double boiler. Add gelatin, let cool Add other ingredients. Pour into molds.

Mrs. D. O. Matthews

White Fruit Salad

1 ½ lb. white seedless grapes, or 2 cans of white cherries

1 large can pineapple

½ lb. marshmallows

½ pint cream, whipped stiff

Dressing:

Cook in double boiler until thick, then cool:

1 egg yolk

Juice of 1 lemon

1 teaspoon prepared mustard

1 teaspoon salt

Dash red pepper

Mix whipped cream with this dressing after it has cooled. Add last to fruit after it has been well drained. Place in the refrigerator for 24 hours before serving.

Mrs. Cora Lee Catchings

Coca Cola® Salad

2 packages cherry Jell-O®

2 bottles Coca Cola®

1 large can Bing cherries

1 large can crushed pineapple

2 pkgs. cream cheese

1 cup nut meats, chopped

Drain juice from cherries and pineapple. Heat juice and pour over Jell-O® to dissolve. Add Cokes®. Halve cherries and remove stones. Chip up cream cheese; add this and other ingredients to Jell-O® when it has thickened slightly. Pour into mold and chill until firm. Serve with baked chicken or turkey.

Mrs. William Peacock

Cranberry Salad

1 lb. cranberries

1-½ cups chopped nuts

¾ cup grated coconut

3 oranges

2 lemons

1-cup sugar

2 envelopes gelatin

Grind cranberries, oranges, and lemons in food chopper. Add nuts and coconut. Boil 1 cup water and sugar. Soften gelatin in 1 cup cold water. Dissolve gelatin in sugar and hot water mixture. Mix with other ingredients and pour into molds.

Mrs. W. G. Sanders

Frozen Fruit Salad

16 marshmallows

2 tablespoons strawberry juice

1-cup crushed strawberries

½ cup crushed pineapple

1 3-oz. package cream cheese

½ cup mayonnaise

1/4 tsp. salt

1-cup cream, whipped

Melt marshmallows and juice in saucepan over low heat, folding until mixture is smooth. Fold in fruit. Blend cream cheese and mayonnaise, then add marshmallow-fruit mixture. Lastly, fold in whipped cream and freeze. Serves 10.

Mrs. Ese Michie

Winter Fruit Salad

2 cups cranberries

½ cup sugar

1 orange

2 or 3 tablespoons mayonnaise

1 small can crushed pineapple

1 cup broken nutmeats

1-cup marshmallows, cut fine

"Mrs. Harry Speakes and Mrs. J. G. Babb were co-hostesses for the business and social meeting of the W. S. C. S. Monday afternoon at the Speakes home, which was bright with arrangements of summer flowers. A large number were present. . . . The hostesses served tomato stuffed with tuna salad on lettuce, open faced sandwiches, devil's food cake and Coca-Cola punch."

—from a local paper clipping in the 1950s WSCS scrapbook

1 package fruit flavored gelatin

Quarter the orange; remove seed and core, leave rind on. Grind with cranberries. Mix all ingredients except gelatin together. Select any flavored gelatin desired and dissolve as directed. Let stand until slightly thick. Fold in other ingredients. Mold as desired. A tart salad delicious with meats or fowl.

Mrs. William Cochran

Frozen Punch

Syrup:

2 ½ cups sugar

2 ½ cups water

Heat until sugar is dissolved. Cool and add to juices.

Juice:

3 pints pineapple juice

Juice of 6 lemons

1 can frozen orange juice

3 cups ginger ale

Freeze. Makes one gallon

Mrs. T. H. Thornton

(original recipe)

Spiced Tea

(Use good, juicy fruit)

4 lemons, sliced very thin

4 oranges, sliced very thin

Add **3 ½ cups sugar** and let it stand for 4 hours. Stir occasionally with a wooden spoon. To **1 gallon boiling water**, add **2 tablespoons tea**, tied loosely in a flour sack; also

1 stick cinnamon

1-teaspoon allspice

Pour this over the first mixture and let this stand 5 minutes only. Then strain through a double cloth similar to flour sack 3 times to make it clear. This is a refreshing drink whether served hot or cold. It can be reheated when ready to serve without changing the flavor.

Mrs. Charles Gramling

Browned Rice

1 can consommé soup
1 cup raw rice
1 cup water
¼ stick oleomargarine
1 medium onion, chopped
Salt to taste

Melt margarine in skillet. Add rice and onion. Cook until rice and onion are well browned. Stir while cooking so mixture does not burn. Put consommé and water into a casserole that can be tightly covered. Add rice to liquid and cover tightly. Bake in a moderate oven until liquid is absorbed. This takes about 35 minutes.

Mrs. O. D. Kitching

Gnocchi of Potatoes

2 lb. potatoes
½ lb. flour
1 egg
Salt

Boil potatoes. Peel and mash well. Cool but don't let them get cold. Sprinkle flour over potatoes. Salt and add egg. Make a dough using a floured board. Cut a piece of dough; roll and cut in 1-inch pieces. Roll in flour; shape in balls. Push dent in each one. Have a large pot of salty boiling water ready; drop the balls in. When they come to the surface, take out. Serve topped with meat sauce as for spaghetti.

Mrs. Max Greganti

Stuffed Cabbage

2 lb. ground round steak
1 lb. rice, cooked
1 large onion or 2 small, finely diced
2 cloves garlic, minced
2 stalks celery, chopped
2 eggs, well beaten
1 large head cabbage
2 cans tomatoes
1 tablespoon sugar
¼ cup cider vinegar
Pinch cayenne pepper
1 teaspoon chili powder
Salt and pepper

Mix together hamburger, rice that has been cooked, onion, garlic, celery, eggs, pinch of pepper, chili powder and salt to season to taste. Boil cabbage in salted water until almost tender, but not falling apart. Fill separate leaves with mixture and make into cigar-like rolls. Put in heavy pan; add tomatoes and enough water to cover rolls. Add **2 bay leaves, pod of garlic, stalk of celery and small onion.** Let come to fast boil, and then turn heat low. Add cayenne and cover. Cook slowly until rolls are done. Add sugar and vinegar when cabbage rolls are nearly done.

Mrs. Donald Kitching

Scalloped Eggplant

Boil **2 medium sized eggplants**. Drain well. Add:

¾ can tomatoes
1 chopped green pepper
4 hard cooked eggs
½ cup onion, chopped
1 tablespoon Worcestershire sauce
¾ cup cracker crumbs
6 crisp slices bacon, broken in pieces, with bacon drippings
(Shrimp can be substituted for bacon)

Salt and add generous dash **Tabasco sauce**. Bake in moderate oven for 30 minutes. Cover with **grated cheese** and run in oven for a few minutes.

Mrs. T. E. (Lexie) Pemble

Lexie Calhoun Pemble was the wife of T. E. Pemble, plantation owner in Merigold. She was related to the former Vice President of the United States John C. Calhoun. She came to Merigold to teach Latin at the high school, and met and married Mr. Pemble. They built a lovely brick house behind the Methodist church, across the street from the Jones house. They were the first household to get air conditioning. Mr. Pemble was a founding member of the Merigold Hunting Club. Stephen and Molly Smith own the house today.

English Peas Casserole

1 medium sized can of English peas
1 cup grated cheese
1 cup cream of mushroom soup, thinned with ½ cup milk
2 pimentos, chopped

Combine all ingredients. Pour into buttered casserole and cook slowly until cheese is melted. Remove from oven.

<u>Topping:</u>

Have mixed ½ **cup grated bread crumbs** and ½ **cup grated cheese**. Sprinkle over the top of peas and return to oven and brown. Serve hot.

Mrs. W. H. (Annie Celeste) Bernard

Asparagus Casserole with Pimento Cheese Sauce

<u>Layer One</u>

3 tablespoons butter
3 tablespoons flour
¾ teaspoon salt
¾ cup milk and ¾ cup asparagus juice, mixed together
Dash of Tabasco sauce
2 chopped pimentos
1 cup grated cheese

Melt butter, stir in flour and salt. Add milk, a little at a time; cook until thick and smooth. Add cheese and pimento.

<u>Layer Two</u>

1 large can asparagus
4 hard boiled eggs, sliced

Use alternate layers of asparagus, eggs, and sauce. Top with grated cheese and cracker crumbs. Sprinkle with paprika. Bake at 400° for 15 minutes.

Mrs. L. T. Michie

Vegetable Casserole

<u>Sauce:</u>

2 cups mayonnaise

1 medium onion, grated

1 teaspoon prepared mustard

8 tablespoons olive oil

1 teaspoon Worcestershire sauce

Dash of Tabasco sauce

Dash paprika

Mix this and keep in refrigerator until needed

<u>Vegetables:</u>

2 ½ cup string beans, fresh or canned

1 pkg. frozen baby lima beans

1 pkg. frozen English peas

Cook and season vegetables separately. Place in layers in casserole or platter while hot. Spread sauce on top. Serve hot.

Geneva Clark

Never Fail Hollandaise Sauce

2 egg yolks

½ teaspoon salt

Dash black pepper

½ cup melted butter or margarine

1 tablespoon lemon juice

Place egg yolks in bowl. Beat well until thick and lemon colored. Add salt and pepper; add 3 tablespoons melted butter a little at a time, beating constantly. Slowly beat in remaining butter, alternately with the lemon juice. Do not cook. Delicious served with asparagus or broccoli.

Mrs. Roger Hall

Jo Mazotti

¼ cup butter or fat

1 ½ lb. ground lean pork (not sausage)

4 large onions, chopped

1 can thick tomato paste

Rinse can with 1 can water

2 ½ cups mushrooms, slices or buttons

1 ½ cup chopped celery

1 cup chopped bell pepper

Salt and pepper to taste

Juice of ½ lemon

3 bay leaves

2 tablespoons Worcestershire sauce

Dash garlic salt

1 lb. sharp cheese, cut into small pieces

Melt fat, add pork, and cook until brown. Cook onions in same skillet until they are clear and golden. Mix meat and onions, and add celery, tomato paste and water, mushrooms, green pepper and remaining ingredients. The cheese is added, too, and cooked with the sauce. Cook about 2 hours very slowly until the sauce is well blended. (I usually make this the day before and put it in the refrigerator.) When you are ready to serve, cook **1 package of broad noodles** until done and combine with the sauce. After these are combined, cook together very slowly about 30 minutes, being careful not to overcook the noodles. This will serve 8 to 12 people, depending on the appetites.

Sue Rayner

Ira Rayner's Chili

1 lb. ground beef (with some fat)

2 large onions, ground

2 bell peppers, ground

1 hot pepper, ground

1 clove garlic, ground

1 tablespoon spice , tied in bag

1 large can tomatoes

2 cans tomato paste

2 tablespoons paprika

Salt to taste

Soak overnight **½ lb. pinto beans** in plenty of water. Cook until half done and add other ingredients. Cook slowly 2 or 3 hours. (This recipe won a prize in *Better Homes and Gardens* magazine.)

Ira C. Rayner, Sr.

Hamburger Corn-Pone Pie

1 lb. ground beef
1/3 cup chopped onion
1 tablespoon shortening
2 teaspoons chili powder
1 teaspoon salt
1 teaspoon Worcestershire sauce
1 cup canned tomatoes
1 cup drained kidney beans
1 cup cornbread batter (1/2 standard cornbread recipe)

Brown meat and chopped onion in melted shortening. Add seasonings and tomatoes. Cover and simmer over low heat for 15 minutes, then add kidney beans. Put in baking dish; top with cornbread batter. Bake at 425° for 20 minutes.

Mrs. Albert Booth, Jr.

Barbecued Chicken Sauce

(Enough for 4 halves)

2/3 cup butter
1 tsp. salt
2 tablespoons flour
2 tablespoons sugar
2/3-cup water
3 tablespoons Worcestershire sauce
1 ½ teaspoons lemon juice
½ cup vinegar
¼ cup vinegar
1/3 teaspoon Tabasco sauce
1/8-teaspoon cayenne pepper

Melt butter over low heat and blend in flour, sugar, salt and water. Cook for a few minutes until salt and sugar are dissolved. Remove from fire and add other ingredients, stirring until all are thoroughly blended.

George G. Cox, Jr.

Stroganoff

1 ½ lb. beef cut in ¾ inch cubes
½ cup chopped onion
1 clove garlic
2 tablespoons fat
Salt and pepper

Flour
1 cup tomato soup
1 16 oz. can mushrooms
1 cup sour cream
6 to 8 drops Tabasco sauce
1 tablespoon Worcestershire sauce
1/8 teaspoon salt

Sauté onion and garlic in fat. Flour meat and brown in vessel with onion; add other ingredients and cook 1 ½ hours at a low heat. This is very nice cooked in a chafing dish; with a salad and dessert it makes a complete meal

Margaret A. Smith

Margaret A. Smith was the second Mrs. Albert Smith (the first Mrs. Albert Smith being the late Velma "Mrs Jiggs" Smith who originated the 1922 cookbook in the first part of this collection). Most in Merigold called her "Aunt Margaret" and there are many delightful stories about her. She was active in the Merigold Methodist Women's Quilting Bee and in its participation in the Crosstie Festival in Cleveland each year. She was an early patron of the arts, giving encouragement and support to Lee and Pup McCarty when they first studied pottery and became artists. The beautiful home and garden that Lee and Pup McCarty developed and where patrons now come from all over the world to shop began as the Smith's mule barn and pasture. She and Albert lived in the white house directly across the street from Merigold United Methodist Church. Dr. Tony Scarborough of Merigold tells this story about Margaret Smith:

"This episode happened a long time ago, maybe around 1975. I cannot be certain of all the dates and exact words. Margaret Smith lived in the house now occupied by Rogers and Mary Helen Varner. "Miss Margaret" had gotten along in years. She loved her home, but was frustrated by the plumbing. There were frequent leaks and drips in toilets, showers, and so on, and she was pretty fed up with plumbers.

"Miss Margaret's health failed and she was confined to Bolivar County Hospital (now Bolivar Medical Center). Her condition worsened. Her family was notified that they needed to start making their way back to Mississippi, as the end was near. Methodist Church ladies found the old choir robes and learned a hymn or two. Certain others prepared food, and they allotted their responsibilities for the funeral.

"And so Miss Margaret died in the hospital. A sheet was pulled up over her. There had been a problem in the bathroom of her hospital room, and a plumber came in and began work on it while they were waiting for the undertakers to come for her. But, miraculously, after some twenty minutes or so, Miss Margaret came back to life, pulled the sheet down from her face, looked over at the plumber in the bathroom, and said, "I'll just be darned. Everywhere I go there's another danged ol' plumber."

"She had undergone what is called a "Near-Death Experience." Miss Margaret later told me that she had been in a beautiful, radiant place with flowers, trees, and wonderfully kind and slightly glowing people. The robed man who welcomed her was patient and kind, as she looked around in awe. He soon explained to her that she would have to go back, but the next time she came she would be allowed to stay. She did not want to return to Earth life and leave the beauty and joy she felt, but had no choice. She awoke on her hospital bed and began breathing again.

"Margaret lived several more years, all of them in eager and confident anticipation of her next, and final, trip to the beyond."

—Dr. Tony Scarborough

Chicken in Cream

1 chicken, cut for frying

Dip in **milk,** roll in **flour** to which **salt** has been added. Fry in **1/3 cup hot fat** until nicely browned. Place in shallow baking dish. Add

1 tablespoon finely chopped onion

1 ½ cup thin cream

Do not cover. Bake in 325° oven for 1 hour.

Mrs. Johnson Barger

Spanish Delight

1 lb. ground beef

2 large onions, chopped fine

1 green bell pepper, chopped

1 can cream style white corn

1 can tomato paste

1 can water

1 can pitted ripe olives

16 oz. pkg. thin noodles

1 lb. Cheddar cheese, grated

1-teaspoon sugar

Salt and pepper to taste

1 tablespoons chili powder

Cook noodles in salted water until almost done. Cook in heave skillet the meat, onions and bell pepper. Add tomato past and water, corn, sugar, chili powder, salt and pepper, olives and lastly, cheese. Reserve part of the cheese to top casserole. Mix noodles and meat mixture together and put in greased casserole. Sprinkle with remaining cheese. Bake 30 minutes in a 350° oven.

Mrs. Joe B. Lee

Barbecued Chicken

3 lb. frying chicken
3 tablespoons shortening
½ cup chipped onion
½ cup chopped celery
½ cup green pepper
2 tablespoons brown sugar
2 tablespoons Worcestershire sauce
1 tablespoon prepared mustard
¾ cup tomato juice
1-cup tomato catsup
¼ cup lemon juice
¼ tsp. pepper
1 tsp. salt
1 clove garlic

Dredge frying chicken in seasoned flour (1/4 teaspoon pepper and 1 teaspoon salt per cup of flour). Fry chicken in deep hot fat until brown. Cook onion, celery, and pepper in fat until tender. Stir in all other ingredients except chicken. Simmer 20 minutes, and then remove garlic. Arrange chicken in 3-quart casserole or large flat baking dish. Cover with sauce. Bake covered for 45 minutes and uncovered for 15 minutes at 350°. Serves 5 to 6 people.

Mrs. J. G. Babb

(Bernice Babb was the wife of the pastor at the time the cookbook was compiled.)

Chicken Casserole

1 large hen, cooked and meat removed from bones
3 cups broth
1 cup rice
1 cup celery, chopped
1 green pepper
2 small cans mushrooms
½ cup chopped almonds
1 large onion, chopped

Cook onion, pepper, celery in chicken fat until tender. Add broth, chicken, etc. Season to taste with salt, pepper, and A-1 Sauce. Cook until all broth is absorbed. Put in casserole, cover with crumbs. Heat when ready to serve.

Mrs. James T. Davis

This is Mari Ana Pemble Davis, only child of T. E. and Lexie Calhoun Pemble of the Pemble Plantation. Mari Ana grew up in the house directly behind and across the street from Merigold Methodist Church. Her mother was a Baptist, while her father was a Presbyterian, influenced deeply by his Presbyterian pastor Dr. Dick Bolling, who had been his pastor in Centreville before they both moved to the Delta. In her mother's later years, Mrs. Davis and her mother attended Merigold Methodist Church because the Baptist church was difficult for Mrs. Pemble to enter due to the high front steps. Today, Mrs. Davis lives in Cleveland but remains active in Merigold life, frequently attending the early worship service at the Methodist church on Sundays and then driving to Cleveland for the 11:00 service at the Presbyterian Church. She graciously gave an afternoon of her time, sharing her photographs and recollections of growing up in Merigold.

Beef and Rice Bake

2 lb. ground beef
½ cup diced green pepper
¼ cup chopped onion
¼ teaspoon pepper
4 teaspoons salt (scant)
1 ½ cups canned tomatoes or 2 cans tomato sauce
3 cups cooked rice (1 cup dry rice, cooked in 2 cups water)

Mix all ingredients and pour into a lightly greased baking dish. Bake in a 375° oven for 1 hour and 10 minutes. This will make 8 to 10 servings.

Mrs. R. H. Howell

Fried Oysters

1 pint oysters

2 eggs, well beaten

1 cup fine cracker crumbs

Hot fat for deep-frying

Drain oysters on paper towel or cloth. Roll oysters in cracker crumbs; dip into egg and again in crumbs. Place in wire basket and fry in deep hot fat until golden brown and crisp. Do not overcook.

Augusta Peacock

Meat Loaf

1 ½ lbs. ground chuck

1 cup bread crumbs

1 onion, chopped

1 egg

1 ½ teaspoons salt

¼ teaspoon pepper

2 tablespoons Worcestershire sauce

½ can tomato sauce

Mix well. Form into a loaf and put into a casserole dish.

<u>Sauce for Top</u>

1 ½ 8-oz. cans tomato sauce

½ cup water

3 teaspoons vinegar

3 tablespoons sugar

2 teaspoons mustard

Pour over top of meat loaf. Bake meat loaf at 375°. Keep it covered for 45 minutes and then uncover it for 20 to 30 minutes, until browned.

Alice Latham

Alice Latham is pictured on the cover, and was the owner of the Merigold Phone Company. She was the mother of Billy Latham.

Meat Loaf

2 lb. ground round steak
1 onion, chopped
1 tablespoon salt
1/2 teaspoon pepper
Dash allspice
Dash cardamom
1 cup bread crumbs
1 egg
2 tablespoons fat
¼ cup water

Combine meat, onion, seasoning, crumbs, and eggs; mix well. Shape into a loaf. Melt fat and pour over loaf. This can be baked in oven or cooked in pressure cooker.

Mrs. E. R. Murphy

Liver Loaf

1 lb. liver
1 onion
1 cup bread crumbs
1 egg
1 cup milk
1 teaspoon salt

Drop the liver in salted boiling water and cook 5 or 10 minutes. Grind in food chopped together with onion. Add breadcrumbs, egg, milk, and salt; mix well. Put in greased baking dish. Set in a pan of hot water and bake ½ hour in 350° oven.

Mrs. Dorothy Hamer

Miracle Rolls

5 cups self-rising flour
1 cup sweet milk
1 cup water
1/3 cup sugar
½ cup shortening
2 yeast cakes

Scald milk. Add sugar and 1 cup water. Let stand until lukewarm. Break yeast cakes into remaining cup water and add 1-teaspoon sugar. Allow to stand while milk is cooling and yeast rises to surface of water. Beat yeast in water and add to milk and water in mixing bowl. Sift in the flour, add shortening, and blend well into dough. Turn out on board and knead a little before returning to bowl. Cover and allow to stand where temperature is about 80 degrees, out of draft, for 30 minutes, then knead again. Roll into 1/2 inch thickness. Cut with small biscuit cutter. Place in well-greased pans and grease

lightly on top. Allow to stand about 20 minutes in warm place. Bake in quick oven (450°
to 500°) for 10 to 12 minutes.

Mrs. Joe King

Hush Puppies

2 cups corn meal
1 cup finely chopped onion
1 cup sweet milk
1 ½ teaspoons salt
1 scant tablespoon baking powder
2 eggs

Sift meal, salt, and baking powder. Then mix in eggs, milk, and onion. Drop in hot deep
fat and cook until brown.

Mrs. Elizabeth King

Quick Buttermilk Rolls

¼ cup warm water (110°-115°)
1 package active dry yeast
¾ cup lukewarm buttermilk
¼ teaspoon soda
1-teaspoon salt
3 tablespoons soft shortening
2 ½ cups sifted flour

In cup, dissolve yeast in water. Stir in buttermilk, soda, sugar, salt, shortening, and half
of flour. Add rest of flour and mix with hand. Turn onto lightly floured board. Knead
until smooth and elastic. Shape and let rise until double (1½ hours). Heat oven to 400°.
Bake 15 to 20 minutes. Makes 1½ dozen rolls.

Mrs. Margie Wade

Brown Bread

2 eggs
1 pkg. dates
1 cup boiling water
2 cups flour
1-teaspoon soda
1-cup sugar
1-tablespoon butter
1-cup nuts
½ teaspoon cinnamon and allspice

Chop dates in large bowl; add soda and boiling water, then butter. Let cook to luke-warm, and then add rest of ingredients. Pour into loaf pan and bake in 350° oven 30 to 45 minutes.

Mrs. W. M. Beck

Banana Bread

2 well-beaten eggs

1 cup white sugar

1-tablespoon sour milk

½ cup margarine or cooking oil

3 mashed bananas

1/8-teaspoon salt

2 cups flour

1-teaspoon soda

Dash of cinnamon

Sift together flour, salt, soda, and cinnamon. Cream shortening and sugar; add eggs and sour milk. Stir in flour mixture, and finally, bananas. Pour into greased loaf pan and bake 1 hour and 10 minutes at 300°.

Mrs. Helen Ward

Apple Pineapple Pie

3 cups pared, diced apples

1 9-oz. can crushed pineapple

1 tablespoon lemon juice

½ teaspoon grated lemon rind

¾ cup sugar

3 tablespoons flour

1 unbaked single-crust pastry

Topping:

½ cup flour

½ cup brown sugar

2 tablespoons melted butter

½ cup chopped nuts

Combine apples, pineapple, lemon juice, and rind. Mix sugar and flour and add to fruit. Put into pastry-lined pan. Blend topping ingredients and sprinkle over fruit. Bake 40 minutes.

Mrs. B. B. Hughes

Bride's Pie

1-cup sugar

3 egg yolks

1-cup milk

1 envelope Knox gelatin, soaked in ¼ cup cold water

1-teaspoon vanilla

1 cup grated coconut

1 cup whipped cream

1 rich pastry crust, baked

Beat sugar and egg yolks, and mix well; bring to boil on slow fire, stirring. Add soaked gelatin; chill. Add vanilla, coconut, and whipped cream. Pour in baked pie shell and congeal.

Sara George Smith

Mock Apple Pie

2 cups water

1 ½ cup sugar

2 teaspoons cream of tartar

Mix ingredients and boil 1 minute. Add **22 Ritz® crackers**. Boil 2 minutes without stirring. Season with **cinnamon and nutmeg** to taste. Pour into **unbaked crust**, dot with **butter** and bake in a moderate oven.

Mrs. Jim Hurd

Southern Pecan Pie

1-cup sugar

4 eggs

1 cup red Karo® syrup

½ stick butter, melted

1 cup pecan halves

Dash salt

1-teaspoon vanilla (optional)

Mix sugar and salt. Add eggs and beat well. Add Karo®, melted butter and vanilla. Pour into raw crust. Place pecan halves on top. Bake in 350° oven for 10 minutes. Reduce heat to 250° and bake for 50 minutes more, or until pie is firm.

Crust for Pecan Pie:

1-½ cups flour

5 or 6 tablespoons fat

1-teaspoon salt

2-½ tablespoons cold water

Cut fat into flour with pastry blender. Stir in water to hold dough together. Knead very lightly to mix well. Chill for a short while, if desired. Roll to 1/8-inch thickness. Place in 9-inch pie pan. Trim and flute edges. This makes pastry for 2 piecrusts.

Mrs. D. L. Bailey and Mrs. A. J. Kelly

Sweet Potato Custard Pie

2 cups cooked sweet potatoes

1-cup sugar

4 eggs

¼ teaspoon nutmeg

¼ stick oleo, melted

1-cup whole milk

Dash salt

Cream potatoes, eggs, and sugar. Add oleo, nutmeg, and salt. Mix well and add milk. Pour in unbaked pie shell and bake at 300° until firm and brown.

Mrs. L. L. Thompson

Chocolate Pie

Crust

1-½ cups flour

¼ teaspoon salt

½ cup Crisco

¼ cup ice-cold water

Add Crisco® to flour and blend thoroughly with a fork. Add the ice water a little at a time and mix well. Roll out on well-floured board into a large circle. Place in pie pan and trim edges. Bake in hot oven until slightly browned.

Filling

1 cup sugar

6 level tablespoons cocoa

½ cup flour

3 egg yolks

2 cups milk

1 teaspoon vanilla

1 teaspoon butter

Mix sugar, flour, and cocoa together. Beat egg yolks slightly and stir into milk. Stir the milk and egg mixture a little at a time into the dry mixture. Blend well. Cook in a heavy saucepan over a low fire. Stir regularly so it will not stick or lump. Remove from heat when smooth and thick. Stir in butter and vanilla. Pour into baked piecrust. Top with meringue made from 3 egg whites. Brown lightly in a moderate oven.

Mrs. James Ollie West

Ambrosia Chiffon Pie

1 pkg. orange Jell-O®
½ cup boiling water
1 cup orange juice
½ cup whipping cream
½ cup powdered sugar
1-½ cups halved seedless red grapes
½ cup shredded coconut
1 9-inch baked pie shell
Membrane-free orange sections

Dissolve Jell-O® in ½ cup boiling water according to directions on package. Add orange juice, chill until syrupy. Beat until light. Beat egg whites, cream, and sugar into gelatin. Chill until almost firm and add 1-cup grapes. Pour into pie shell. Sprinkle with coconut. Garnish with orange sections and remaining grapes. Chill until firm.

Mrs. Robert Hawthorne

Lemon Icebox Pie

½ cup lemon juice
2 egg yolks
1 can sweetened condensed milk

Combine lemon juice, egg yolks, and condensed milk until well blended. Pour into a crust of **crushed vanilla wafers**. Make a meringue of the **2 egg whites and 5 tablespoons of sugar**. Bake in a hot oven until the meringue is brown.

Mrs. Steve Johnston

Chess Pie

4 whole eggs
1 ¼ cups sugar
½ cup butter
1-cup milk
1-tablespoon flour

Slightly beat egg. Blend sugar with eggs. Add milk and butter and beat well. Add flour to thicken. Pour into unbaked pie shell and bake until thickened, so that knife blade comes out clean.

Ida Newby

Lemon Chiffon Pie

(Filling for one 9-inch pie)

1 envelope Knox sparkling gelatin

¼ cup cold water

4 eggs

1-cup sugar

½ cup lemon juice

½ teaspoon salt

1 teaspoon grated lemon rind

Add ½ cup sugar, lemon juice, and salt to beaten egg yolks and cook over boiling water until of custard consistency. Soften gelatin in cold water. Add to hot custard and stir until dissolved. Add grated lemon rind; cool. When mixture begins to thicken, fold in stiffly beaten egg whites to which the other ½ cup sugar has been added. Fill baked pie shell or graham cracker crust and chill. Just before serving, spread over pie a thin layer of whipped cream.

Mrs. Sidney Lee

Parfait Pie

2 whole eggs

1 cup sugar

1 13 oz. can evaporated milk

1 ½ cups pineapple juice

1 box orange gelatin

Mix the eggs, sugar and pineapple juice. Cook until it thickens. This will be about the thickness of soft custard. Add gelatin and cool. Whip the evaporated milk that has been thoroughly chilled in the refrigerator. Add the cooked mixture to the whipped milk. Pour into a baked pie crust of a vanilla wafer crust. Refrigerate for at least 2 hours before serving.

Mrs. Joseph Oliver

Cherry Angel Pie

1 #2 can (2 ½ cups) unsweetened cherries

1 tablespoon (1 envelope) unflavored gelatin

¼ cup cold water

Cherry liquid, plus water to make 1 cup

2 tablespoons lemon juice

¼ cup confectioners sugar

1 cup heavy cream, whipped

Drain cherries. Soften gelatin in cold water. Heat cherry liquid to boiling. Stir in sugar. Add gelatin mixture, then lemon juice. Chill until partially set. Fold confectioners sugar into whipped cream. Fold into gelatin mixture, and then fold in cherries. Pour into meringue crust.

Meringue crust:

> 2 egg whites
> 1/8-teaspoon cream of tartar
> 1/8-teaspoon salt
> ½ cup sugar
> 1 teaspoon vanilla.

Mix egg whites with cream of tartar and salt. Beat until stiff. Beat in sugar gradually until mixture forms very stiff peaks. Fold in vanilla. Spread on bottom and sides of a 9-inch greased pie pan. Put a portion of the meringue through pastry tube to form fancy edge on crust. Bake in 300° oven for about 45 minutes. Cool.
Chill the whole pie thoroughly before serving.

Mrs. L. O. Deweese

Jellyroll

> 5 eggs, separated
> 1-cup sugar
> 1 ½ cups flour, sifted
> 1-teaspoon vanilla
> 1 teaspoon lemon juice
> Jelly

Beat 5 egg whites. Add yolks, unbeaten and beat 5 minutes more. Add sugar and beat five minutes. Fold in flour, vanilla, and lemon juice. Bake in a jellyroll pan and turn out on damp cloth sprinkled with sugar. Spread jelly on while hot and roll up in towel. Serve with cream sauce or thin sauce with orange peel flavor.

Mrs. Robert A. Hall

Cream Puffs

(Good and Easy to Make)

> ½ cup shortening
> 1-cup hot water
> 1 cup sifted all-purpose flour
> ¼ teaspoon salt
> 4 eggs

Put shortening and water in small saucepan and heat to boiling point; add the flour and salt which have been sifted together. Beat until it is smooth and pulls away from sides of pan. Then, add the eggs one at a time, beating thoroughly after each. Drop dough with tablespoon onto a baking sheet. The mixture should hold its shape and not run together. Bake in a hot oven about 10 minutes about 425° or 450° the reduce heat to 400° and continue baking for about 25 minutes. When cooled, fill with the following filling:

>5 tablespoons flour
>
>½ cup sugar
>
>Pinch salt
>
>2 cups sweet milk
>
>2 slightly beaten eggs

Add milk gradually at first to insure against lumps. Blend and cook gently over boiling water until thickened. Let cook. Continue to stir so a "skin" will not form over the top. When cool, add **vanilla and almond extract to suit taste (about 1 tablespoon vanilla and ½ almond)**. Whip until stiff, **½ pint whipping cream**. Add **5 tablespoons sugar**. Fold this into the custard mix. Split the cooled cream puff near the top and fill with the creamed custard. Press the top over the filling and sprinkle with **powdered sugar**.

>Mrs. W. L. Malley

German Chocolate Cake

>1 pkg. German's sweet chocolate
>
>½ cup boiling water
>
>1-teaspoon vanilla
>
>1 cup Crisco
>
>2 cups sugar
>
>4 egg yolks, well beaten
>
>1-cup buttermilk
>
>2 ½ cups sifted cake flour
>
>1-teaspoon soda
>
>4 egg whites, well beaten

Melt chocolate in boiling water. Add salt after chocolate melts. Cream shortening and sugar. Add beaten egg yolks; add alternately ¾ cup buttermilk and flour. Dissolve soda in remaining buttermilk and add to creamed mixture. Stir in melted chocolate. Fold in egg whites. Bake in three 9-inch cake pans in 350° oven for 25 to 30 minutes.

>Icing:
>
>1 tall can evaporated milk
>
>1 stick oleomargarine (1/2 cup)
>
> 2 egg yolks
>
>1-cup sugar
>
>1 cup chopped pecans
>
>1 cup Angel Flake coconut

Mix milk, sugar, egg yolks, and oleomargarine. Remove from fire and add coconut and pecans. Cool enough to spread.

>Mrs. J. S. Fincher and Mrs. J. R. McDonald

Orange Chiffon Cake

Use level measurements throughout. Sift an ample amount of good cake flour onto a square of paper. Sift together into a mixing bowl:

> 2 ½ cups flour
>
> 1 ½ cup sugar
>
> 3 teaspoons baking powder
>
> 1-teaspoon salt

Make a well in center and add in the following order:

> ½ cup cooking oil
>
> 5 unbeaten egg yolks
>
> Juice of 2 medium-sized oranges, plus enough water to make ¾ cup
>
> Grated rind of the 2 oranges (about 2 tablespoons)

Beat with a spoon until smooth. Measure into another mixing bowl:

> 1-cup egg whites (7 or 8)
>
> ½ teaspoon cream of tartar

Beat until whites form very stiff peaks. They should be much stiffer than for angel cake or meringue. Do not under beat. Pour egg yolk mixture gradually over the egg whites, gently folding with a rubber scraper just until blended. Do not stir. Pour into an <u>ungreased</u> pan immediately. Bake in a 10-inch tube pan at 325° for 65 to 70 minutes, or until top springs back when lightly touched. Immediately turn pan upside down, placing tube over the neck of a bottle or funnel until cake is cold. Loosen from sides and around tube with spatula. Turn pan over and hit edge sharply on table to loosen.

<u>Filling:</u>

Melt in pan **½ cup butter or oleomargarine,**; remove from heat and blend **in 4 tablespoons cake flour and ¼ teaspoon salt.** Stir in slowly **½ cup orange juice**. Bring to a boil, stirring constantly. Boil one minute. (If mixture curdles, do not be alarmed). Remove from heat and stir in **3 cups sifted confectioners sugar**. Set in pan of cold water. Beat until of spreading consistency. Stir in **2 tablespoons grated orange rind**. Ice the cake.

Sidney G. Cox

"The Women's Society of Christian Service met in the home of Mrs. E. B. Hill for the last lesson in the study of Paul's Letters to the Local Churches. After the devotional the leader, Mrs. Harry Speakes presented the interesting study. The hostess served **orange chiffon cake,** fudge squares, and coffee during the social hour."

Chocolate Fudge Cake

1-cup sugar

½ cup butter

3 eggs

2 squares bitter chocolate, melted

¾ cup flour

1-teaspoon vanilla

1-cup pecans

Cream butter and sugar. Beat eggs until light and add to creamed mixture. Stir in melted chocolate, then mix in flour; add vanilla and pecans. Bake in a greased and floured loaf pan in slow oven. Delicious sliced and served with a scoop of vanilla ice cream on top.

Mrs. E. B. Blanchard

Fruit Layer Cake

3 cups flour

2-½ cups sugar

½ cup butter

1-cup seedless raisins

1-cup jam

1-cup buttermilk

1-teaspoon soda

1-teaspoon each allspice, cinnamon, and nutmeg

6 eggs

Cream butter and sugar. Sift flour and spices together. Add soda to buttermilk. Add beaten eggs to creamed mixture, and then add alternately milk and flour.   Add raisins and jam. Bake in 3 layers in 375° oven.

Filling:

1-cup sweet milk

1-cup coconut

1-cup seedless raisins

1 cup chopped pecans

2 cups sugar

1-tablespoon flour

1-jar maraschino cherries

2 eggs

Mix all ingredients together and cook until thick. Spread between layers and on top and sides. Cake is better when stored a week or so.

Mrs. Hugh Marberry

Cherry Cake

1 #2 can red-pitted cherries, drained with juice reserved

1 ½ teaspoon cornstarch

½ cup sugar

Mix the cherry liquid, cornstarch, and sugar and cook slowly until thick. Cool and add

1 teaspoon almond extract

Cake Dough:

½ cup butter

1-cup sugar

2 eggs

2 cups flour

½ teaspoon salt

2 teaspoons baking powder

1-teaspoon vanilla

Mix ingredients well to form dough. Press half of dough into 9 x 13 inch pan. Spread with cherries and thickened juice. Cover with other half of dough.

Topping:

2 tablespoons melted butter

¼ cup sugar

¼ cup flour

¼ cup chopped pecans

Mix well and sprinkle on top of cake. Bake in 350° oven for 1 hour.

Annie N. Adelson

Applesauce Cake

1 can or 2 cups applesauce

2 teaspoons soda

2 eggs

½ cup cooking oil

2 cups sugar

4 cups flour

1-cup seedless raisins

1 -cup chopped dates

1 -cup chopped nuts

1-cup fig preserves

1-cup watermelon rind preserves

2 teaspoons cinnamon

2 teaspoons cloves

2 teaspoons allspice

1-teaspoon nutmeg

Mix applesauce and soda until soda stops foaming. Roll dates, nuts, and preserves in half the flour. Add other ingredients. Bake in a greased stem pan in 300° oven for about 2 hours. Garnish cake with **nuts and cherries**.

Mrs. Tressie Wood

"The Business and Social meeting of the Woman's Society of Christian Service was held in the home of Mrs. Ed Rayner, Monday afternoon, with Mrs. Albert Booth, Sr., Mrs. W. M Beck, and Mrs. Albert Booth, Jr. as co-hostesses. Lovely pink roses decorated the reception rooms, and centered the dining room table . . . . The guests were invited into the dining room where the table was draped with linen and centered with lovely pink roses. Mrs. Charles Lawrence presided at the silver coffee service, while Mrs. Robert Gramling served strawberry shortcake from a silver platter. Other appointments held salted nuts, and marshmallows."

—from a local paper clipping in the 1950s WSCS scrapbook

Prune Cake

3 eggs

2 ¾ cup strong coffee

3 cups flour

2/3 cup butter or margarine

1 ½ cup sugar

1 teaspoon cinnamon

1 teaspoon mace

1 ½ teaspoon soda

1 cup pitted prunes (boiled 10 minutes)

Cream sugar and shortening and add beaten eggs. Beat well. Sift flour and dry ingredients except ½ teaspoon soda. Add ½ teaspoon soda to hot coffee and let cool; add pitted prunes to the creamed mixture. Add flour and coffee alternately. Bake in moderate oven.

Frosting:

1 ½ boxes confectioner's sugar

Enough evaporated milk to make spreading consistency

¼ stick margarine

1 egg white

Mix all ingredients until well blended.

Mrs. D. A. Yarborough

Upside Down Pineapple Cake

3 eggs, separated

1 cup white Karo®

5 tablespoons pineapple juice

1-cup flour

1-teaspoon baking powder

Mix all ingredients together except egg whites. Beat these very stiff and fold into cake batter. Cream **together 1 cup brown sugar and ¼ cup margarine**

Line a heavy skillet with this mixture. Place **drained pineapple slices, maraschino cherries and pecans** in this sugar mixture. Pour cake batter into skillet. Bake 40 minutes at 300°. Let cool and turn out on cake plate. This cake may be served plain or with whipped cream.

Mrs. Lucille Wells

One Two Three Four Cake

1 cup shortening

2 cups sugar

3 cups cake flour

4 eggs

1-cup milk

1-teaspoon salt

2 teaspoons baking powder

2 teaspoons vanilla

Sift flour, sugar and salt together. Mix cake with electric mixer. Blend in shortening on low speed to corn meal consistency. Add eggs on medium speed, one at a time; add milk and flavoring. Increase to highest speed. Use a rubber spatula to keep batter moving from side to center. When smooth, reduce to low speed and add baking powder. Blend well, but do not beat long. Bake in two 9-inch cake pans in 375° oven for 35 minutes. Cake may be baked in loaf pan in 325° oven.

Caramel Icing:

Melt **½ cup butter**. Add **1-cup brown sugar**, firmly packed. Cook until blended and slightly thickened; stir constantly. Cool slightly and add **¼ cup milk**. Beat until smooth. Gradually beat in **2 cups sifted confectioners sugar**.

Mrs. C. R. Riley

Jam Cake

Cream together

    ½ cup butter

    1-cup sugar

    3 egg yolks

Add

    1-cup jam

    1-teaspoon allspice

    1-teaspoon nutmeg

    1-teaspoon cloves

    1-teaspoon cinnamon

Add alternately

    2 cups flour

    ½ cup buttermilk

Add

        3 stiffly beaten egg whites.

Add (dissolved)

        1-teaspoon soda

        1/3-cup hot water

Bake in layers and frost with your favorite icing or bake into a loaf or muffins. Bake in moderate oven 20 minutes for layers or 45 minutes for loaf.

        Mrs. C. F. Kittle

Mincemeat Cake

½ cup shortening
1-cup sugar
1 teaspoon vanilla
Pinch salt
3 eggs
1 ½ cups buttermilk
1 ½ teaspoons soda
3 teaspoons baking powder
1 cup prepared mincemeat
1 cup chopped pecans
Flour to make thick batter

Cream sugar and shortening; add salt, vanilla, and eggs. Beat well. Add buttermilk. Sift together 1 cup flour, soda and baking powder. Add to creamed mixture. Add mincemeat and pecans. Add enough flour to make thick batter. Recipe makes four 9-inch layers. Bake in greased and floured pans in moderate oven. Frost with caramel icing.

        Mrs. W. O. Ragsdale

W.S.C.S. Christmas Party

The lovely home of Mrs. Ed Rayner was the setting for the Christmas program for the WSCS on Monday, December 17, with Mrs. O. D. Kitching and Mrs. Alice Latham as co-hostesses. The Rayner home was never more beautiful than on this occasion with its colorful Christmas decorations from the entrance through the rooms open to the guests. Claiming attention in the living room was the pretty mantel arrangement. At one end of the mantel was placed a miniature choir, with tiny white tapers lighting the scene, while tall white candles burned at the other end surrounded by angel hair and tiny green balls. Above the mantel hung a gold wreath tied with colored ribbons. On the coffee table stood a tiny tree, the branches of which were tied with Christmas balls. Beneath the tree greeting cards were prettily arranged. On occasional tables were large red candles nestled on beds of holly. The beautifully decorated Christmas tree stood at the entrance to the sun parlor forming a pretty picture with its glittering ornaments.

The president, Mrs. Lawrence, presided over the meeting and welcomed the large number of members and guests. After the roll call and minutes, the treasurer gave her report showing a tidy sum in the general fund. After a business session Mrs. Charles Lawrence presented the well-planned program. Mrs. W. O. Hunt read the scripture and with Miss Sue Rayner at the organ, Mary Hull sang several Christmas carols. The meeting closed with prayer, after which the guests were invited into the dining room where glowing red tapers lighted the scene. On the buffet stood Santa's white reindeer, flanked by candelabra holding light tapers and also on the serving table burning tapers were grouped. The refreshment table was centered with silver branched candelabra, decorated with clusters of various colored Christmas balls. On the table were **trays of ribbon sandwiches, salted nuts, stuffed dates, and crackers.** Mrs. Lawrence served **congealed salad** from a crystal tray at one end of the table; Mrs. Hunt poured **coffee and hot chocolate** from the other end. The guests passed into the living room for the social hour.

—from a local paper clipping in the 1950s WSCS scrapbook

Fruitcake

2 cups applesauce

2 teaspoons soda

1 egg

1 cup butter or cooking oil

2 cups sugar

2 cups raisins

4 cups flour

1 cup chopped dates

2 cups chopped nuts

2 cups mixed candied fruit

2 teaspoons cinnamon

2 teaspoons allspice

1 teaspoon nutmeg

Sift flour and spices together. Add fruit. In separate bowl, mix applesauce, soda, egg, melted butter or oil, and sugar. Combine all ingredients. Pour into well-greased and floured tube pan and bake in slow oven (300°) about 2 hours.

Mrs. H. E. Browning

Banana Nut Cake

3 cups flour

2 teaspoons soda

½ teaspoon salt

1½ teaspoon cinnamon

1½ teaspoons allspice

1½ teaspoon cloves

2 cups pecans

1 cup raisins

1 cup chopped dates

6 large bananas, mashed

4 eggs

2 cups sugar

½ cup cooking oil

¼ cup butter or margarine

Cream oil, sugar, and margarine. Stir in eggs and bananas. Add 1 ½ cups flour, spices, salt, and soda. Take 1 ½ cups of flour and roll raisins, nuts and dates. Add to mixture and bake in a slow oven, about 300° for 1 hour and 20 minutes. Bake in large tube pan.

Mrs. J. R. Herrington
Mrs. J. S. Hawkins
Mrs. W. A. Kelly
Mrs. R. I. McLemore

Date Fruit Cake

Prepare fruits and nuts the day before you plan to use them. Also line 4 loaf plans with 2 layers of greased brown paper and on layer of greased wax paper. Place the following into a bowl:

>8 cups chopped pecans
>1 lb. candied pineapple, cut into small pieces
>1 lb. candied cherries, quartered
>2 lb. snipped dates

Put into sifter:

>3 cups sifted flour
>2 teaspoons baking powder
>2 teaspoons salt

Sift into nut and fruit mixture. Mix slowly together with spoon until all nuts and fruit are covered. In another bowl, place

>8 whole large eggs

Beat until well blended. Blend in

>2 cups sugar, added one at a time.

Add

>3 tablespoons vanilla extract
>1 tablespoon almond extract

Pour liquid over nut-fruit mixture. Blend with spoon until well blended. Pour into prepared pans and bake for 1½ hours at 250°.

Mrs. Hoyt Daves

Master Butter Cake

>1 cup shortening
>2 cups sugar
>4 eggs, beaten
>1 ½ cups milk
>2 teaspoons vanilla
>4 cups flour
>½ teaspoon salt
>4 teaspoons baking powder

Cream shortening and add sugar gradually. Continue creaming until fluffy. Add eggs. Beat until light. Sift flour, measure and add salt and baking powder; sift again. Add dry and liquid ingredients alternately. Beat until thoroughly blended. Bake in four 8-inch pans or 1 big round pan at 370°.

Mrs. Ethel Wachter

Feather Devil's Food Cake

½ cup lard
1 cup white sugar
1-cup brown sugar
1-teaspoon vanilla
2 beaten eggs
3 1-oz. squares unsweetened chocolate
½ cup hot water
2 cups flour, plain or cake
¼ teaspoon soda
2/3 cup sweet or sour milk

Thoroughly cream lard and sugar; add vanilla and eggs. Beat until fluffy. Melt chocolate in hot water; blend and cool slightly. Add to creamed mixture. Add flour, sifted with salt and soda, alternately with milk, beating well after each addition. Place batter in 2 greased 9-inch layer pans. Bake at 350° for 30 minutes.

Mrs. Harry Speakes

Ethelyn Fincher Speakes's husband managed the branch of the Cleveland State Bank in Merigold, and he also assisted his father, Mr. Earl Speakes, who owned and operated a grocery story in downtown Merigold on the block where Crawdad's is today. Mr. Speakes came home to eat dinner every day and expected to have it served to him promptly at 12:00 noon. Mrs. Speakes cooked in the tradition of her mother, Mrs. Gertie Fincher, serving at least one meat and five or six bowls of vegetables and bread. Mr. Harry expected her to have a pie baked for his lunch everyday, too.

Her son, Larry recalled this about his parents: "My mother was big with the Women's Society of Christian Service. My Dad would never come early to church. He said there was too much standing up and sitting down for the songs. After church, my mother would linger with her friends. My dad and I went straight home because a big chicken dinner was waiting. Finally, my dad would say, 'We'll have to get the key to the church to get her out.'"

Larry Speakes also remembered growing up near the church, the parsonage, and the park. He said, "Growing up, our house was next to the Methodist preacher. His name was Brother Guinn. He made a big garden back behind the parsonage and wore jodhpurs. I believe he  *was a bachelor. We had a pear tree close to the fence between our house and his. We told him he could have all the pears on his side of the fence.*

The Baptist parsonage was just across the street. Later, Brother Sturdivant was the Baptist preacher. He played volleyball with us often. He was boisterous, and when his side was winning, he would say, 'The Giants are Marching!' We always thought that the park was the 'Center of the Universe.'"

From the *Bolivar Commercial*, Monday, November 23, 1981, page 6:

Church Women's Quilt Travels to White House—

The Merigold United Methodist Church Women recently completed a patchwork quilt, which will hang in the White House in Washington. Mrs. E. D. Rayner made and designed the top for the colorful quilt. The quilt will travel to Washington on request of former Merigold resident Larry Speakes, Deputy Press Secretary, in Washington. The result of the women's combined efforts will be on display with other Mississippi mementos in the White House. Larry Speakes is the son of Mrs. Harry Speakes. Pastor of the Merigold United Methodist Church is the Rev. Bo Mills.

Refrigerator Fruit Cake

32 marshmallows
1½ lb. graham crackers
1½ pint xx cream (leave in ice box overnight)
¼ cup sweet pickle juice or wine
½ teaspoon cinnamon
½ teaspoon nutmeg
1 cup chopped dates
1 cup pecans
1 cup raisins
1 cup currants
¼ cup chopped figs
½ cup candied pineapple, red and green
¾ cup candied cherries
¼ cup citron
2 tablespoons shredded orange peel

Roll graham crackers into small pieces. Whip cream and add to it marshmallows and pickle juice or wine. Let this stand while preparing other ingredients. Wash raisins and currants and pour boiling water over them, allowing enough to cover. Put aside to soak and soften. Put crackers and spices into a large bowl and mix thoroughly. Add pineapple, cherries, and citron. Drain raisins and currants; roll in a tea towel. Add to cracker mixture, using a wooden spoon to stir. Add cream and marshmallows and stir as long as you can and then use hands.

When thoroughly mixed, put into loaf or stem pan that has been lined with 2 sheets of heavy oiled paper. Pack mixture compactly pressing in corners and center with palm of hand. Decorate with nuts, cherries, and pineapple. Let stand in refrigerator 24 hours.

Mrs. Albert Booth, Sr.

Thumbprint Cookies

½ cup shortening
¼ cup brown sugar
1 egg yolk
½ teaspoon vanilla
1cup flour
¼ teaspoon salt
1 egg white
¾ cup finely chopped nuts (pecans are best)
Tart jelly

Mix shortening, sugar, vanilla, and egg yolk. Sift salt and flour together. Stir into creamed mixture. Make very small balls of dough (about 1 teaspoon). Roll in egg white and then in nuts. Bake on un-greased cookie sheet at 375° for 5 minutes. Remove from oven and thumbprint indentation in the center of each. Return to oven for 8 to 10 minutes more. When done, fill centers with jelly while cookies are warm. Makes about 2 dozen.

Mrs. Ernest Meek

Dedication of the New Organ at Merigold Methodist Church

A grand service of dedication was held at Merigold Methodist Church for the new organ on a Sunday afternoon in 1955. A newspaper clipping from the local paper reports that the service included organ solos by Miss Sue Rayner, Mrs. Louise Hall, Mrs. R. M James, and Mrs. Clifton Langford. Vocal selections were presented by Mrs. Billy Smith of Shelby and Mrs. James Milstead of Cleveland. The Rev. Dr. Richard A. Bolling of the Presbyterian Church in Cleveland gave a memorial address remembering the life of Lucy Park. The paper also reports that "A reception was held in the recreation room of the church, which for the occasion, was beautifully decorated. The long refreshment table, covered in an imported white cutwork cloth, edged in lace held as its center decoration a silver epergne holding pink and white gladiolas and candytuft flanked by branched silver candelabra with lighted white tapers. At the two silver coffee services placed at either end of the table were Mrs. W. O. Hunt, wife of the pastor, and Mrs. Wroten, wife of the district superintendent.

Apricot Horns

1 lb. butter or oleomargarine

1 lb. creamed cottage cheese

4 cups sifted flour

Blend ingredients together to form a dough. Add more flour if cheese is watery. Shape into 1-inch balls and refrigerate overnight. Dough may be kept under refrigeration for a month.

<u>Filling:</u>

1 lb. dried apricots

2 cups of sugar

Cook apricots until tender, drain, and puree. Add sugar while they are still hot; allow to cool.

<u>Coating :</u>

1-½ cups ground almonds

1 ¼ cups sugar

2 egg whites, slightly beaten

Confectioner's sugar

Mix sugar and nuts. Roll each dough ball into 3-inch rounds, making only 10 horns at a time so dough will stay cool. Place 1 teaspoon of apricot filling in center of the pastry. Roll up in shape of a horn. Dip in egg white, and then roll in nut mixture. Place on greased cookie sheet. Bake in 375° oven for 12 minutes, or until lightly browned. Sprinkle with confectioners sugar. Yields about 11 dozen.

The crust is delicious to use as a piecrust as well.

Mrs. Mattie Hollinsworth

Starlight Mint Surprise Cookies

½ lb. chocolate mints

1 cup shortening

¾ cup sugar

1 egg

2 ¼ cups flour

1 ½ teaspoon baking powder

¾ teaspoon salt

1-tablespoon light cream

1-teaspoon vanilla

Cream together sugar and shortening; beat in egg. Sift together flour, salt, and baking powder. Put vanilla in cream; add flour mixture and cream to creamed mixture. Shape cookies by enclosing a half chocolate mint in about 1 teaspoon of dough. Place on greased baking sheet 2 inches apart. Top each cookie with walnut half or pecan or colored sugar. Bake in moderate oven.

Mrs. H. E. Ramsey

Oatmeal Cookies

3 cups oatmeal

1 cup brown sugar

1 cup flour

1 cup margarine, melted

1-teaspoon vanilla

1-teaspoon soda

3 tablespoons hot water

1 cup chopped nuts

Mix oats, sugar, and flour. Stir in margarine, then nuts. Dissolve soda in hot water and add to other mixture. Make into a long roll; put on waxed paper in the refrigerator. Let stand until firm. Slice thinly and bake in 375° oven for about 12-14 minutes. Don't crowd on the cookie sheet because they spread. This recipe freezes well before baking.

Mrs. Alice Latham

Chinese Almond Cookies

4 cups self-rising flour

½ teaspoon baking powder

2 cups shortening

2 cups sugar

1 egg, beaten

2 tablespoons almond extract

1 teaspoon almond extract

1 teaspoon vanilla extract

Sift together flour and baking powder. Add shortening, sugar, egg and 2 tablespoons almond extract; mix well. Add 1 teaspoon almond extract and vanilla. It is easier to use hands to mix this. When thoroughly mixed, take a heaping teaspoon of dough and roll ball between palms of hands. Place on an un-greased cookie sheet. Pat ball slightly flat with fingers. Press 1 blanched almond into center. Cookies may have a "cracked" appearance after doing this. Place cookies about 1-½ inches apart on cookie sheet. Bake in 325° oven for 12 to 15 minutes, or until golden brown. Let cookies cool on cookie sheet for a few minutes and remove with a spatula. Makes about 5 dozen.

Mrs. Hugh Wun

"On Monday afternoon the Woman's Society of Christian Service met in the home of Mrs. J. P. McLaurin. . . . Bright fall flowers were used in the living and dining rooms. . . Plans were discussed for the family night to be held on the sixteenth at Merigold Methodist Church. The supper will honor the members of the Merigold School Faculty. . . . The hostesses served stuffed tomatoes, crackers, pickles, cookies, and iced tea."

Fig Bars

½ cup shortening

¾ cup sugar

1 egg

½ teaspoon baking powder

2 cups flour

¼ teaspoon salt

1teaspoon vanilla

½ teaspoon grated orange peel

3 tablespoons milk

Cream shortening and sugar. Add egg and beat well. Add vanilla and orange peel. Sift flour with salt and baking powder. Add alternately flour and milk. Roll out; cut in 3-inch strips as long as possible. Spread with fig filling and cut into 2-inch lengths. Bake in 350° oven about 20 minutes.

Fig Filling

1 can of canned figs

½ cup sugar

2 tablespoons flour

Mix together and cook about 5 minutes, or until thick. Cool.

Mrs. Donald Yarborough

Refrigerator Pinwheels

1cup butter or margarine

1cup white sugar

1cup brown sugar

3 eggs

1teaspoon vanilla

4 cups flour

1teaspoon soda

½ teaspoon salt

Cream butter until soft; add sugar and continue creaming. Add eggs and vanilla. Beat until light. Add flour, soda, and salt. Roll dough and spread with filling.

Filling:

1 lb. dates, run through food chopper

½ cup orange juice

1cup nuts

½ cup sugar

Combine ingredients and cook until thick. Cool and spread on rolled dough as for jelly-roll. Wrap in waxed paper and chill overnight. Cut in slices and bake in moderate oven.

Mrs. Frank Jones

Toffee Cookies

1 cup oleomargarine
1 cup brown sugar
1 egg, separated
1 teaspoon vanilla
2 cups flour
½ teaspoon salt
2 teaspoons cinnamon
½ cup ground nuts

Cream oleomargarine and sugar. Add unbeaten egg yolk and vanilla. Sift flour, salt, and cinnamon together; add slowly to creamed mixture. Pat out to about ½ inch thickness. Spread beaten egg white on top and sprinkle with nuts. Bake in 275° oven for about 30 minutes. After baked and cool, cut into squares and lift out with spatula.

Mrs. Bernard Adelson

By Cracky Bars

Sift together:

1 ¾ cups sifted flour
1-teaspoon salt
¼ teaspoon soda

Blend together:

¾ cup shortening
1-cup sugar

Cream well. Add

2 eggs

Beat well and combine

1/3-cup milk
1-teaspoon vanilla

Add alternately with dry ingredients to creamed mixture. Place 1/3 of batter in second bowl. Add

1 square (1 oz.) melted chocolate
¾ cup pecans, chopped

Spread into well-greased 13 x 9- inch pan. Arrange **9 double graham crackers** over batter in pan. Add **¾ cup semi-sweet chocolate pieces** to remaining 2/3 of batter. Drop by spoonfuls over graham crackers and spread to cover. Bake in moderate oven (375°) for 20 to 25 minutes. Cut into bars when cool.

Mrs. H. C. Burrus

Loganberry Ice Cream

1 can sweetened condensed milk
2 cups loganberry juice or other berry juice
Juice of 1½ lemons
2 egg whites
1 cup undiluted milk, chilled

Mix condensed milk, loganberry juice, and lemon juice; pour into freezing tray. When partly frozen, remove to chilled bowl and whip until light and fluffy. Return to tray; when partly frozen, remove and heat again. Then fold in stiffly beaten egg whites and whipped evaporated milk. Freeze until firm, stirring once.

Mrs. J. C. Hallman

Lime Cherry Sherbet

1 4-oz. jar maraschino cherries, chopped
3 cups sugar
1 ¼ cups lime juice
2 quarts whole milk
Few drops green food coloring

Combine sugar and lime juice; add milk gradually. Stir in cherry syrup. Add food coloring. Stir in chopped cherries. Freeze in gallon ice cream freezer.

Mrs. Clay Rayner

Cheese Cake

(Makes 2 pies)

1 cup boiling water
1 pkg. lemon Jell-O®
34 graham crackers
1 stick oleomargarine
¼ cup sugar
1 large or 2 small pkg. cream cheese at room temperature
1 large can Pet® milk
1 cup sugar

Mix 1 cup boiling water in lemon Jell-O.® Roll out or crush 34 graham crackers. Mix in ¼ cup sugar, then add 1 stick melted margarine. Use ½ of crumb mixture for bottom crust of pies. Grease bottom of pans first. Whip 1 large can chilled Pet milk until stiff. Mix in 1-cup sugar. Add lemon Jell-O®, cream cheese and vanilla. Cover top of pies with remaining crushed crackers. Chill before serving.

Mrs. Warren T. Gray

Ruth's Steamed Pudding

1½ cups butter

1 cup sweet milk

1 cup molasses

1 teaspoon soda

2 cups flour

1 ½ cups raisins

1 cup chopped pecans

1 teaspoon cinnamon

Mix all ingredients together. Steam in a casserole for 3 hours.

Sauce

½ cup butter

1 cup sugar

1 egg yolk

¾ cup boiling water

1 beaten egg white

Cream butter; add sugar, and egg yolk. Slowly stir in water. Cook a few minutes. Add beaten egg white to sauce before removing from fire. To serve, pour sauce over pudding and top with whipped cream flavored with vanilla or whiskey. Top this with grated co-conut.

Mrs. Ruth Locke's recipe
given by Mrs. T. E. Pemble

"Top of the Barn" Cobbler

Sift together:

½ cup sugar

½ cup flour

1 ½ teaspoon baking powder

Add **1/3 cup milk**. Melt **1 stick of margarine** in pan; pour in batter. Add **fruit** (any kind, raw or cooked), do not stir. Bake 45 minutes at 350°. Serves 6. Serve hot or cold. Good with whipped cream or ice cream.

Mrs. "Pup" McCarty

Pup McCarty was the wife of Lee McCarty and one of the potters of Merigold. The title of the recipe comes from the fact that Lee and Pup's home was upstairs in the renovated mule barn that once belonged to Albert and Margaret Smith in downtown Merigold, where the McCarty's started making ceramic art in 1948.

Strawberry Preserves

2 quarts berries, washed and blanched with 2 quarts hot water in colander. Lift out. Do not add water. To the berries, add **4 cups sugar**. Let come to boil and boil 5 minutes, then add **4 more cups of sugar** and boil 15 minutes. Let set overnight and can next morning.

Mrs. J. P. McLaurin

Never Fail Divinity

2 cups sugar
½ cup corn syrup
½ cup water
Dash salt

Stir all ingredients together. Boil gently to 240° or soft ball stage. Gradually pour 1/3 corn syrup over 2 stiffly beaten egg whites, beating constantly. Cook the rest of the syrup to 265° or hard ball stage. Wipe off any sugar crystals on sides of pan. Beat syrup into candy mixture. Continue beating until mixture holds its shape. **Add 1 teaspoon vanilla**. Drop by spoonfuls on greased cookie sheet.

Mrs. Charles Lawrence

Chocolate Candy

2/3 cup cocoa
3 cups sugar
2 tablespoons white corn syrup
¼ teaspoon salt
1 ½ cups milk
4 ½ tablespoons butter
1 teaspoon vanilla

Mix cocoa, sugar, and salt. Stir in milk and syrup. Bring to boil, stirring frequently. Cook to 232°, or until a small amount of mixture forms a soft ball when dropped in cold water. Remove from heat; drop in butter. Cool to lukewarm; add vanilla and beat until mixture thickens. Pour into buttered pan and cut into squares. One cup nuts may be added after the vanilla.

Mrs. M. D. Underwood

Date Loaf

3 cups sugar

2 tablespoons Karo® syrup

1 cup chopped pecans

2 teaspoons vanilla

1 ½ cups milk

1 box seedless dates, chopped

½ teaspoon salt

1 tablespoon butter

Mix together sugar, syrup, and milk. Cook until it forms a soft ball in water. Add dates. Stir well. Add salt, butter and vanilla. Beat until creamy, add nuts. Pour onto a wet tea towel. Roll and let cool. Unwrap and slice.

Mrs. T. Coffman

Buttermilk Fudge

2 cups sugar

2 tablespoons Karo®

1 cup buttermilk

1 teaspoon soda

1 stick oleo or butter

3 cups chopped pecans

Stir soda into the buttermilk; add sugar and Karo®. Put in large saucepan and cook until it comes to a boil. Drop in a stick of butter and continue to cook to the soft ball stage. Remove from heat and beat until creamy. Add chopped pecans and drop by spoonful onto waxed paper or greased cookie sheet. Yields 1 lb.

Mrs. Calvin Campbell

Recipes from "The Groaning Board"

Today's Merigold Cooks
and the
United Methodist Church's
First Wednesday Potlucks

The Merigold First Wednesday Potlucks

The weekly quilting bee begun after the 1970 census eventually evolved into a community-wide potluck lunch held at Merigold United Methodist Church on the first Wednesday of each month. One can stop by at noon on the first Wednesday and find friends and neighbors not only from the church but from many different churches, and not only from Merigold, but from all around the county, entering the side door of Merigold United Methodist Church laden with casseroles, meats, vegetables, salads, and desserts. When the group has assembled, dishes have been uncovered, serving spoons have been placed in each dish, china plates, some chipped now from years of use, have been

stacked at the head of the food table and a sweating glass of ice water is at each place around the tables, Cack Meyer calls the group to order, shares a brief devotional thought, asks for prayer concerns from the community, and calls on the pastor to ask a blessing on the feast spread on what has become known as the "groaning board," a table so heavily laden with deli-

cious food that it "groans." Any first time visitors get to go through the buffet line first,

but after the first visit, they become one of the group. Diners gather around the tables and catch up on each other's lives and children and grandchildren. Recipes are discussed and shared. New dishes tried by cooks for the first time are critiqued and complimented. Children crawl on the smooth wooden floor and play with wooden blocks, plastic tea sets, and metal toy trucks in the adjacent playroom and nursery. It

161

is a place where all are welcomed and where all leave well-filled with some of the best comfort food anyone could imagine enjoying. Some must rush back to the office or to the field, while others linger a little longer to hear one more funny story or share one more recollection of days gone by. The community has grown a bit closer and no one feels quite as alone as before.

Christmas at Merigold UMC

Several years ago, Jim Meyer began locating and bringing a large fresh cut Christmas tree and putting it up in the middle of the fellowship hall in mid-December, a tree so tall that it had to be cross anchored from the second floor balcony that runs around the perimeter of the room. Children and adults would come together for a sumptuous potluck meal and work together to decorate the massive tree. This tradition continues.

A unique addition to the 2009 gathering was the presence of a contingent of fire-fighters from Poland who were visiting Bolivar County, exchanging information with our firefighters. These guests attended the fourth Sunday of Advent Christmas worship, followed by the large meal and tree decorating. Although there was a bit of a language barrier, the international language of music, food, and love were eloquently spoken. A local television station covered the event for the evening news.

Appetizers, Sauces, Beverages, and Finger Foods

Hot Chocolate Mix

*(This is a regular feature of the coffee hour that immediately follows
Sunday morning worship at Merigold.)*

1 lb. box Nestle Quik® (more if you like)

1 lb. box confectioners sugar

½ lb. Coffeemate® creamer

1 8 qt. box nonfat dry milk.

Mix all this together. I do this in my food processor in batches and then mix together in a large container. This makes 1-gallon dry mixture. To serve, add 1 cup boiling water to 4 tablespoons mix.

Sue Rayner Latham

Spiced Tea Mix

1/2 c. instant tea

2 ½ cups sugar

2 cups Tang®

2 small pkgs. lemonade

2 teaspoons cinnamon

1 teaspoon cloves

Mix all ingredients and store in airtight container. To make a single serving, add boiling water to 3 teaspoons mixture in mug.

Monica Parker

Russian Tea

3 qts. water

3 cups sugar

1 teaspoon allspice

1 teaspoon cloves

1 stick cinnamon

Juice from 8 oranges

Juice from 6 lemons

2 cups pineapple juice

5 tea bags

Mix water and sugar and let come to a boil. Add spices in a cloth and let simmer for 10 minutes. Add tea bags and simmer 5 minutes. Remove tea bags and spices. Add juices and heat. Do not allow to boil. Serve hot.

Renelda Owen

Shrimp Sandwiches

2 cans small shrimp
1 celery stick, finely chopped
1 cup mayonnaise
6 oz. cream cheese
½ teaspoon mace
¼ teaspoon dry mustard
½ teaspoon onion juice
Salt and Tabasco to taste

Mix well and serve on crackers or cut into party sandwiches.

Karen Brunetti

Ham & Cheese Party Rolls

1 ½ sticks margarine, softened
3 teaspoons mustard
3 teaspoons poppy seeds
2 tablespoon minced onions (optional)
1 teaspoon Worcestershire sauce
8 oz. shredded or thinly sliced ham
8 oz. shredded mozzarella cheese
4 oz. shredded cheddar cheese
2 pkgs. Dainty Dinner rolls

Mix together first 5 ingredients. Slice across rolls to make one large top and bottom. Spread butter mixture on each half; place ham on half of bread, then top ham with cheese. Top with the other half of the bread. Wrap in foil and bake at 350 degrees 30 - 45 minutes. Can be made the night before - be sure to allow a little extra cooking time.

Jennifer Cleary

Cheese Straws

½ lb. sharp Cheddar cheese, grated
1 stick butter, (not margarine)
1 ½ cup plain flour
½ teaspoon salt
1/8 teaspoon red pepper

(I use the processor to make these.) Grate the cheese on the grater blade. Soften the cheese and butter at room temperature whil you get the flour, etc. together. Mix cheese and butter with the steel blade—add 1 cup of the flour and mix. Add the other ½ cup flour, salt, and red pepper. Process until it forms a ball. Using the "star" blade of a cookie press, put on cookie sheet. Bake in 375 ° for 12 to 14 minutes. Watch closely as there is nothing worse tasting that over-cooked cheese. Store in a tin box. Keeps well and it is not necessary to freeze.

Sue Rayner Latham

Pizza Squares

1 can pizza dough
1 cup mayonnaise
1/4 cup parmesan cheese
14 oz artichokes (drained & chopped)
1 cup shredded mozzarella cheese
1 small jar sundried tomatoes in oil
   (w/garlic)
2 tablespoons cornmeal

Spray cookie sheet with Pam® (Olive Oil or regular) and sprinkle cornmeal on pan (shake all over). Spread pizza dough and mash to sides. Mix other ingredients and spread over dough. Bake at 425 for 12 to 15 minutes. Cut into squares.

Susan processes artichokes and sun dried tomatoes in processor. I chopped artichokes and tore tomatoes into bite-size pieces. It was wonderful.

Linda Hiter

Cheese Snaps

2 sticks margarine
2 cups grated sharp cheese
2 cups Rice Krispies® cereal
Dash onion salt
Dash Tabasco
1/4 teaspoon garlic salt
2 cups flour

Soften margarine and mix in cheese. Add flour and mix. Add remaining ingredients. Roll into balls and press on cookie sheet. Bake at 350° for 15 minutes.

Monica Parker

Mushroom Cups

18 slices white bread
½ lb. chopped fresh mushrooms
3 tablespoons finely chopped green onions
½ stick butter
2 tablespoons flour
½ pint whipping cream
½ teaspoon salt
¼ teaspoon cayenne pepper
5 teaspoons chopped frozen chives
1 tablespoon chopped parsley
1 teaspoon lemon juice
1 tablespoon each brandy and sherry
Parmesan cheese

Bread cups: Preheat oven to 350°. Roll bread slices to flatten. Use small biscuit cutter to cut 2 circles from each bread slice. Press into small muffin pan. Bake until toasted, about 10 min. Remove to cookie sheet.

Filling: Saute onions and mushrooms in butter for 10 – 15 mins. Sprinkle in flour. Stir. Add cream, stir at low boil until mixture thickens. Remove from heat, add herbs and seasonings. Spoon mixture into bread cups. Sprinkle with parmesan cheese. Bake at 350° until bubbly.

To Freeze: Leave cup on cookie sheet and put in freezer. When frozen, remove from cookie sheet and place in plastic bags. Return to freezer. Reheat frozen cups 10 mins. At 350°.

This recipe was given to me by Rayner Sessions Christopher when she lived in Merigold. Rayner used Oyster mushrooms grown by her company, Merigold Mushroom Company.

Louise Meyer

Teena Hemphill's Remoulade Sauce

2 egg yolks
½ pint Creole mustard
¼ cup vinegar
Juice of one lemon
Salt and pepper to taste
1 pint oil

Blend all ingredients except oil. Add the oil to the mixture slowly, continuing to blend. Serve over shrimp on a bed of lettuce.

Sue Rayner Latham

Dill Sauce

Dr. Henry Outlaw, retired chemistry professor at Delta State University who lives in Meri-gold, brings this delicious sauce to accompany his smoked pork tenderloin when we have our monthly potluck lunches. It is wonderful.

1/3 cup mayonnaise
1/3 cup horseradish
2 tablespoons lemon juice
1 teaspoon dill (dried or fresh)
Paprika to taste (optional)

Mix and chill. Serve to accompany meats or fresh vegetables.

Henry Outlaw

Pumpkin Dip

1 (8-ounce) block cream cheese, softened
1 jar marshmallow cream
1/2 of a (12-ounce) can pumpkin pie filling
1/4 teaspoon nutmeg
1/4 teaspoon cinnamon

Combine all ingredients, mixing well. Serve with gingersnaps.

Renelda Owen

Artichoke Dip

1 tall slender can grated Parmesan cheese
2 cans artichoke hearts, drained
1 pkg. Italian salad dressing mix (dry)
1 pint jar mayonnaise
½ cup sour cream

Mix all ingredients and process well in blender. Refrigerate. Serve with Melba toast, crackers, or corn chips.

Cack Meyer

Marinated Shrimp with Artichoke Hearts

2 lbs. shrimp, peeled
1 purple onion, sliced thin
1 ½ cups oil
1 ½ cups apple cider vinegar
½ cup lemon juice
1 jar marinated artichoke hearts
1 to 2 teaspoons celery seed
1/3 cup sugar
½ teaspoon salt
1 ½ tablespoons capers
1 ½ tablespoons Tabasco
1 bay leaf

Mix well and refrigerate overnight.

Karen Brunetti

Margaret Smith's Sardine Dip

1 can "good" sardines
Onion, finely chopped
2 tsp. lemon juice
¼ teaspoon Tabasco
Mayonnaise

Drain sardines and mash thoroughly with a fork. Add an equal amount of finely chopped onion. Add lemon juice and Tabasco. Add enough mayonnaise to blend all this together. This recipe yields about ½ cup dip. Chill well and serve with saltines.

Sue Rayner Latham

Sausage-Rotel® Dip

1 lb. sausage, cooked and drained
1 lb. Velveeta cheese, cubed
1 can diced Rotel® tomatoes

Mix cooked sausage and cubed cheese in a double boiler and stir until melted. (You may choose to do this step in microwave.) Add tomatoes and mix thoroughly. Serve with corn chips.

Sue Rayner Latham

Vidalia Onion Dip

2 Vidalia onions chopped
3- 8oz. pkgs. cream cheese
2 cups Parmesan cheese
½ cup mayonnaise

Mix all ingredients together and bake in serving dish 425° for 15 minutes. Serve with Triscuit® crackers.

Linda Hiter

Three-Layer Cheesecake

3 8-oz. packages cream cheese, softened and divided
3 tablespoons chopped pimento-stuffed green olives
2 teaspoons olive juice
1 tablespoon mayonnaise
1 cup (4 oz.) shredded sharp Cheddar cheese
1 (2 oz.) jar diced pimiento, drained
1 teaspoon grated onion
1 cup butter or margarine, softened
2 garlic cloves, pressed (or, ¼ teaspoon garlic powder)
1 teaspoon dried Italian seasoning

Allow cream cheese to come to room temperature. Beat 1 package of the cream cheese at medium speed with an electric mixer until creamy; stir in olives and juice. Spray 8"x4" loaf pan with cooking spray and line with plastic wrap. Spread olive mixture in pan for first layer. For layer 2, beat 1 package cream cheese at medium speed until creamy; add mayonnaise and Cheddar cheese and process until blended. Stir in the pimento and onion. Spread over the olive layer in the pan. For layer 3, beat remaining package of cream cheese and butter at medium speed until creamy; add garlic and Italian seasoning, beating until blended. Spread garlic mixture over pimiento layer. Garnish with parsley around the loaf, if desired. Cover and chill at least 3 hours or until firm. Serves 8 for appetizers. (I do each step in my food processor using the steel blade. I let it "firm up" between layers.) I like to place loaf on an oblong plate and serve with Wheat Thins or other assorted crackers and fresh fruit, if desired. This keeps well and can be patted back into a loaf shape as needed, if you are patient. This makes a pretty presentation and is not as much trouble as you would think.

Sue Rayner Latham

Black-Eyed Pea Dip

1 medium onion, chopped
2 tablespoons butter
15 oz. can black-eyed peas, washed and drained
14 oz. can artichoke hearts, chopped
1 can Rotel® tomatoes
2 tablespoons Parmesan cheese

Mix well. Refrigerate 2 to 3 hours. Serve with corn or tortilla chips.

Karen Brunetti

Reuben Dip

8 oz. cream cheese, softened
½ cup sour cream
1 tablespoon ketchup
2 teaspoons minced onion
2 teaspoons brown mustard
1 cup sauerkraut, drained, chopped
½ lb. corned beef, chopped fine
1 cup grated Swiss cheese

Preheat oven to 375°. Stir together cream cheese, sour cream, ketchup, onion and mustard until well blended. Stir in sauerkraut, corned beef and Swiss cheese; mix well. Transfer to small, ovenproof casserole, cover, bake for 30 minutes. Uncover, bake 5 min more or until begins to turn golden. Serve with rye crackers or pita chips.

Louise Meyer

Breakfast and Brunch Dishes

Swiss Eggs

1 tablespoon butter

½ cup sour cream

4 eggs

Salt, pepper, and cayenne to taste

2 tablespoons grated Velveeta® cheese

Melt butter and add the cream. Slip in eggs gently and add seasoning. When egg whites begin to set, add the grated cheese. Serve on buttered toast with cream poured over eggs.

Park Hiter

Baked Grits

1 cup cooked grits

1 roll garlic cheese

1 stick butter

3 eggs

Milk

Salt to taste

Grated sharp Cheddar cheese for topping

Beat eggs in measuring cup with fork until well blended. Add enough milk to make 1 cup liquid. Mix with hot grits. Add butter and cheese that has been cut up. Stir over low heat until melted. Put into buttered casserole and top with grated cheese. Bake at 350° for 45 minutes to 1 hour. Let stand about 5 minutes before serving. Serves 8 to 10.

Sallie Meek

Brenda Heflin's Cheese Grits

1 cup grits

4 cups water

1 ¼ teaspoons garlic salt

1 stick margarine

6 oz. Velveeta cheese

2 eggs, beaten well and enough milk

to make 1 cup

Cook grits in water and garlic salt. Add remaining ingredients and mix. Pour into a greased casserole dish and bake at 350° about 25 minutes or until firm.

Sausage-Cheese Grits

4 cups water
1 cup quick grits, uncooked
2 cups (8 oz.) grated sharp Cheddar cheese
¼ cup milk
2 tablespoons margarine
2 teaspoons Worcestershire sauce
1 ½ teaspoons garlic salt
1 egg, beaten
1 lb. hot bulk pork sausage, cooked and drained
1 cup (4 oz.) grated sharp Cheddar cheese

Bring water to a boil in a large saucepan; stir in grits. Return to a boil; cover, reduce heat and cook for 5 minutes, stirring occasionally. Remove from heat and add 2 cups grated cheese and next four ingredients, stirring until the cheese melts. Stir in a small amount of grits mixture into beaten egg; adding remaining grits mixture slowly.

Spoon half of grits mixture into a lightly greased 9 x 13 casserole; top with sausage. Spoon remaining grits mixture over this. Cover and chill for 8 hours.
To bake: remove from refrigerator and let stand at room temperature for 30 minutes. Bake uncovered at 350° for 40 minutes. Sprinkle with 1 cup cheese and bake for 5 more minutes.

Sue Rayner Latham

Christmas Morning Breakfast Casserole

1 lb. sausage, browned and drained
2 cups milk
6 slices bread, without crust, cubed
4 eggs, beaten
1 teaspoon salt
1 teaspoon dry mustard
½ lb grated cheddar cheese
1 can sliced mushrooms, optional

Place bread in 13" x 9" glass dish. Top with cheese, sausage, and mushrooms. Mix milk, eggs, salt and mustard and pour over bread. Refrigerate at least twelve hours. Bake at 325° for 1 hour, covered. Serves 6 to 8. Serve with stewed dried fruit and blueberry muffins for a complete meal.

Virgie "Tutter" Jones White

Bacon Quiche

1 cooled pastry shell (baked at 425 for 6-8 minutes)

4 eggs, beaten

2 c. half and half

3/4 tsp. salt

1/4 tsp black pepper

12 slices bacon, fried and crumbled

1/2 c. grated Swiss cheese

1/2 c. grated mozzarella cheese

Sprinkle bacon and cheeses over bottom of pastry. Mix eggs, half and half, salt and pepper. Pour into pastry. Bake at 425° for 15 minutes. Reduce heat to 300° and bake an additional 40 minutes.

Monica Parker

Cheesy Ham and Artichokes
(This is good for brunches)

4 tablespoons butter

4 tablespoons. all-purpose flour

2 cups warm milk

Dash of seasoned salt

Dash of Cayenne pepper

1/4 teaspoon ground nutmeg

Paprika

Dash of white pepper

2/3 cup shredded Swiss and Parmesan cheese, mixed for sauce

4 tablespoons sherry

2 (1 lb.) cans artichoke hearts, drained

12 thin slices boiled or baked ham

2/3 cups shredded Swiss and Parmesan cheese, mixed for topping

2/3 cup bread crumbs for topping

Melt butter in saucepan; blend in flour. Over low heat, stir in milk gradually until thickened. Add seasonings and cheese; stir over low heat until melted. Remove from heat; stir in sherry. Cut artichokes in half and wrap two halves in a slice of ham. Arrange in buttered casserole with sides touching; pour sauce over all. Sprinkle cheesy bread crumbs topping over casserole. Bake at 350° for 25 to 30 minutes.

John Taylor (from Mary Alice Taylor)

Soups and Salads

Cack's Salad Dressing

(Used for many years at Crawdad's Restaurant in Merigold)

1/3 cup sugar

1/3 up red wine vinegar

2/3 cup canola oil

Salt and pepper to taste

Shake or mix sugar and vinegar until sugar is dissolved. Add oil slowly until slightly thick. Add salt and lots of pepper. Recipe can be doubled and stored in refrigerator.

Cack Meyer

Dobbs House 1000 Island Dressing

¾ cup dill pickle relish

½ cup sweet pickle relish

4 hard-cooked eggs, chopped

½ cup stuffed olives, chopped

2 pimentos, chopped

1 quart mayonnaise

Salt to taste

Chili sauce to taste

Mix and add chili sauce to the color you like.

Renelda Owen

Frozen Salad

1 cup water

1 cup sugar

1 12-oz. can orange juice concentrate

1 16-oz. can apricots, drained and cut up

1 20 oz. can crushed pineapple

6 bananas, cut up in pieces

Make a simple syrup of the water and sugar and then cool. Mix all ingredients together and freeze in paper cups supported in a muffin pan. Makes about twenty ½ cup servings. Keep stored in a zipper bag in the freezer. This is very refreshing and good to have on hand for "Boo" company.

Sue Rayner Latham

Salad for the Bereaved

1 can cherry pie filling
1 un-drained can crushed pineapple (20 oz.)
1 can condensed milk
2 teaspoons almond flavoring
Juice of 2 lemons
1 12 oz. Cool Whip
Toasted slivered almonds

Mix together and freeze in paper muffin cups; makes about 2 dozen cups. You can add a drop of red food coloring if you like. This is Clemmie Griffin Collins' recipe. She says to keep this made and frozen so that when there is a death in the community, *you are ready*. Then after you use this, make another one and you will be "ready" next time.

Sue Rayner Latham

Cranberry Salad

1 lb. fresh cranberries, chopped finely
1-cup fruit cocktail
1-cup coconut
1-cup pecans
2 cups sugar
1 cup whipping cream, whipped until firm

Mix all ingredients well and chill.

Sally Jo Lishman

Lime Congealed Salad

1 small pkg. lime Jello®
8 oz pkg. cream cheese
1 c. hot water
1 small can crushed pineapple (drained)
1 c. pecans
1 c. mayonnaise

Dissolve Jello® in hot water. Add remaining ingredients. Pour into 9 X 11 pan or Jello® mold and chill overnight.

Monica Parker

Corn Salad

1 12 oz. can whole kernel corn, drained
1 cup finely chopped celery
1 cup chopped green bell pepper
2 tsp. prepared mustard
¼ cup pimento, chopped
3 T. salad oil
½ teaspoon each salt and pepper
Enough mayonnaise to moisten, about 1 tablespoon

Combine all ingredients and chill until served.

Mitsi Meyer

Grand Old Opry Salad

1 teaspoon pepper
1 tablespoon water
½ cup oil
1 teaspoon salt
¾ cup vinegar
1 cup sugar
1 cup chopped purple onion
1 large bell pepper, chopped
1 can French style green beans, drained
½ package frozen peas
1- 16 oz. can shoe peg corn, drained
1 cup chopped celery
1–3 oz. jar chopped pimento

Mix pepper, water, oil, salt, vinegar, and sugar. Boil for five minutes. Mix the other ingredients in a mixing bowl and pour the boiled mixture over vegetables. This salad will keep refrigerated for 2 weeks. Good with everything.

Virgie "Tutter" Jones White

English Pea Salad

2 cups canned English peas
½ cup diced cheese
½ cup chopped sweet pickles
¼ cup chopped pimento
1 tablespoon minced onion
2 hard cooked eggs, diced
¼ cup salad dressing
Salt and pepper

Mix and chill.

Louise Meyer

Tutter's Oriental Slaw

½ red cabbage, chopped
½ green cabbage, chopped
½ bunch green onions, chopped
½ cup celery, chopped

Mix above and set aside

1 package Ramen noodles
1 cup chopped pecans
½ stick butter

Sauté noodles and pecans in butter. Drain on paper towel.

Dressing:
1-cup oil
½ cup sugar
½ cup red wine vinegar
3 teaspoons soy sauce
Salt and pepper to taste

When ready to serve slaw, put the amount of dressing you want on cabbage mixture and top with noodles and pecans. Don't add the noodles and pecans until ready to serve and then only add the amount that will be eaten right away.

Virgie "Tutter" Jones White

Jennifer's Oriental Slaw

2 packages beef flavored Ramen noodles
2 packages coleslaw (in cello bag already shredded)
½ cup slivered almonds, toasted
½ cup sunflower seeds

Marinade

¾ cup sugar
1 cup oil
½ cup red wine vinegar
2 packages of flavor mix from noodles
1 tablespoon Worcestershire
1 tablespoon soy sauce

Mix marinade and heat until sugar dissolves. Let cool. Set aside. Cook noodles as directed (break into smaller pieces before adding to water). Drain, rinse in cool water to stop cooking. Chill. Mix with slaw, add nuts. Pour marinade over all, stirring to mix well. Chill at least 2 hours.

Jennifer Cleary

Sue Latham's Potato Soup

1 ½ lb. potatoes
1 ½ cups water
½ cup celery
½ cup onion
10 oz. chicken broth
1 small can evaporated milk
2 cubes chicken bouillon
1 tablespoon butter
Salt and pepper to taste

Place first four ingredients in pot. Cook until vegetables are done. Add remaining ingredients and simmer a few minutes.

Nell Pitts

"My" Stew

1 ½ lbs. stew meat or chuck roast, cut into 2" chunks
Flour, salt and pepper for dredging
1 beef bouillon cube
Oil for browning
2 ½ cups water
1 8-oz. can tomato sauce
5 carrots
4 medium potatoes
2 large onions

Flour and season 1- 1 ½ lbs. stew meat (I buy a chuck roast and cut it in about 2" chunks) with salt and pepper and 1 beef bouillon cube. Brown meat in a small amount of oil in a heavy pot. Add 2½ cups water. Cook slowly for 2 hours. Add tomato sauce; rinse can with water. Add carrots cut into chunks. Add potatoes, cut into chunks and then add the onions, cut into chunks. Don't add the vegetables until stew is almost through cooking.

Sue Rayner Latham

Mimi's Tomato Soup

1 quart jar tomatoes
1 quart jar water
1 cup milk
1/4 stick oleo or margarine
1/8 tsp. baking soda
2 T. flour
Salt and pepper to taste.

Mix together and simmer. Do not boil!! Serve with cornbread. You can also add diced onions when serving.

Monica Parker

"My" Mushroom Stew

1 ½ lb. pkg. Mushrooms, cleaned and sliced
½ stick margarine
1 bunch green onions, cleaned and sliced,
            including some of the green tops
¼ cup flour
1 14-oz. can chicken broth (*not* fat free)
2 soup cans milk
5 chicken bouillon cubes

Sauté mushrooms and onions with margarine in a heavy pot. Work in flour. Add broth and milk. Heat slowly over low flame. Add bouillon cubes. Do not boil this soup—simmer slowly.

Sue Latham

Side Dishes

Jenny Smith's Asparagus Casserole

    1 can cream of mushroom soup
    2 cans asparagus, undrained
    1 can asparagus, drained
    1 tablespoon chopped onion
    1 tablespoon grated cheese
    1 raw egg
    ½ cup mayonnaise
    Melted butter
    4 slices white bread, untrimmed

Mix onion, cheese, egg, and mayonnaise together well. Add soup. Put asparagus into a greased casserole dish and top with sauce. Dip white bread in melted butter and lay across the asparagus and sauce. Bake about 25 to 30 minutes at 350°.

Sue Rayner Latham

Stuffed Mushrooms

Whole mushrooms, 3 or 4 per person. Remove stems, wash, and pat dry. Keep in a plastic bag until ready to prepare. The day before, prepare mixture and refrigerate overnight:

1 minced onion

2 tablespoons melted butter

¼ cup flour

½ teaspoon salt and pepper

½ cup milk

½ cup sour cream

1 egg

1 box chopped spinach, cooked and water squeezed out

¼ cup crisp bacon, crumbled

Sauté onions in melted butter. Cook until tender. Add rest of ingredients. Refrigerate overnight. Next day, dip mushrooms in melted butter. Stuff with spinach mixture. Top with **Parmesan cheese**. Bake at 350° for about 20 minutes. This is a great accompaniment to steak or crown pork roast.

Virgie "Tutter" Jones White

Turnip Greens

6 to 8 bunches mustard greens

1 lb. bacon

large sweet onion, cut in 1/4" slices

Thoroughly wash greens, removing stems and large veins. Chop in 1-2 inch pieces. Fry one pound bacon in large pot. Remove bacon, retaining grease. Cook onions in bacon grease until brown. Remove onions. Add greens to grease, turning to coat leaves. Add bacon and onions. If liquid is needed, add chicken stock to cover greens. Cook on low heat for approximately 3 hours.

Mike Parker

Green Bean Bundles

1 can whole green beans, drained

1 pkg. bacon

Italian dressing

Garlic salt

Parmesan cheese

Roll three to four green beans in a strip of bacon for an individual serving. Insert toothpick to hold. Place on a baking pan or dish. Pour small amount of Italian dressing over beans. Sprinkle garlic salt and Parmesan cheese on top of each. Bake at 400° until bacon is done.

Mitsi Meyer

Stir-Fried Green Beans

1 lb. package frozen cut green beans
¼ cup olive oil
2 tablespoons butter
½ teaspoon chopped garlic
4 to 5 slices onion
½ teaspoon sugar
1-teaspoon salt
½ teaspoon black pepper

Place green beans in a bowl. Cover with boiling water. When beans have thawed, drain. In a stir-fry skillet, add oil, butter, garlic, and onions. Cook until onions are limp. Add green beans. Turn quickly until beans are coated with oil mixture. Add more oil, if needed, to be sure beans are covered. Add the sugar, salt and pepper. Stir often until beans are done. ¼ cup of water can be added if needed. Cover to hurry cooking.

Cack Meyer

Three-Bean Casserole

1 can French-style green beans
1 can lima beans
1 can sweet peas
1 cup mayonnaise
1 small onion, chopped
1 teaspoon Worcestershire
3 boiled eggs, chopped (optional)
1 teaspoon Tabasco
1 tablespoon Wesson oil
¾ cup Croquets
1 can French Fried Onion Rings.

Drain the three cans of beans. Mix them with the mayonnaise, onion. Worcestershire, eggs, Tabasco, oil and Croquets. Put in a casserole dish, and bake at 350° until it bubbles. Add fried onion rings. Run in oven and heat. (I omit the eggs.)

Brenda Outlaw

Baked Beans

1 lb. can Bush Original Baked Beans®
1 small onion, thinly sliced
2 slices bacon, cut in 1" pieces
2 tablespoons catsup
1 tablespoon packed dark brown sugar
¼ teaspoon dry mustard
1 tablespoon barbecue sauce (I use Corky's®)

Mix beans, catsup, sugar, mustard, and barbecue sauce together. Pour ½ of mixture into casserole. Cover mixture with thin sliced onions. Add rest of mixture. Top with bacon pieces. Cover and cook for 45 minutes at 375°. Uncover and cook about 30 minutes.

Cack Meyer

Merigold Tomatoes

2 (14 oz.) cans tomato wedges, or peeled, diced tomatoes
¾ cup chopped onion
¾ cup bell pepper
1 tablespoon brown sugar
1 ½ teaspoons Lea and Perrins® Worcestershire
Dash of Tabasco
¾ teaspoon Cajun seasoning (like Tony Chachere's®)
1 bag or box of Pepperidge Farm Stuffing®

Sauté onion and bell pepper until tender. Add to tomatoes with the seasonings. Add 1 cup stuffing mix; salt and pepper to taste. Spoon into greased casserole dish. Cover and bake for 30–35 minutes in a 350° oven.

Virgie "Tutter" Jones White

Tesi's Corn Rice Casserole

1 16 oz. pkg. yellow rice mix
1 can undiluted cream of chicken soup
1 12 oz. can Mexicorn®
1 cup grated Cheddar cheese

Cook rice as directed on package. Add soup and Mexicorn®. Pour into buttered casserole dish. Top with grated cheese. Bake at 350° for 25 to 30 minutes. This is Caleb's favorite!

Mitsi Meyer

Buz and Rebecca Peeples' Indian Corn Pudding

2 (14 ½ oz.) cans cream style corn
1 cup stone ground yellow corn meal
½ cup oil
1 large egg, slightly beaten
1 tablespoon garlic salt
1 cup grated Cheddar cheese
1 cup green chilies (1 can)

Mix all together and bake 1 hour at 350°

Millie Allen

Spanish Vegetable Casserole

3 cans whole kernel corn
3 cans English peas
1 large can mushrooms
1 can pimento, chopped
1 can mushroom soup
1 stick butter

Drain vegetables and save liquid. Sauté mushrooms in butter. Add vegetables and simmer in Dutch oven for 30 minutes. Add pimento. Blend mushroom soup with drained vegetable liquid and add to vegetables. Bake at 350° until bubbly.

Mary Katherine Lawrence

Marinated Vegetables

1 can tomato bisque
1/2 cup salad oil
3/4 cup salad vinegar
1/2 cup sugar
1 teaspoon mustard
1 teaspoon black pepper
1 bag carrots, sliced and cooked
1 cup whole green beans, drained
1 cup English peas
1 red onion, ringed
1 green bell pepper, ringed

Mix first six ingredients and pour over vegetables. Refrigerate overnight, stirring occasionally.

Monica Parker

Sweet Potato Casserole

5 large cooked and mashed sweet potatoes
1 stick butter
1 cup firmly packed brown sugar
Mix all together and bake in casserole dish at 350° for 25 to 30 minutes.
Mitsi Meyer

Old Fashioned Sweet Potato Pudding
"My Fair Lady"

2 eggs
1 cup sugar
2 cups grated raw sweet potatoes
2 cups milk
1 stick butter
Nutmeg to taste
Pinch of salt

Beat eggs, add sugar, and then mix with remaining ingredients. Place in a buttered casserole and bake at 350° for 45 minutes to 1 hour.
Jean Weatherly

Scalloped Pineapple

9-11 fresh bread cut in cubes
20 oz. can pineapple chunks
½-1 can crushed pineapple
3 eggs
2 cups sugar
2 sticks butter

Preheat oven 350°. Grease 9 x 12 glass casserole dish, place bread cubes and pineapple. Melt butter; add sugar, and eggs and pour over pineapple and bread. Bake 350° for 45 minutes to 1 hour. Delicious! Men love it!!

Corn Bread Dressing

1 8" to 10" skillet of cornbread
2 or 3 slices of white bread
1 cup chopped onion
1 cup chopped green pepper
1 cup chopped celery
4 cups chicken broth
Salt, pepper, and sage to taste

Crumble corn bread and white bread. Sauté vegetables in cooking oil until semi-soft. Add broth and heat. Pour mixture over breads. (Add more broth as needed.) Season with salt, pepper, and sage to taste. Bake in 350° oven 10 or 12 minutes.

Mary Katherine Lawrence

Squash Dressing

1 medium onion
¼ lb. margarine
2 cups cooked squash
2 eggs
1 (10 ¾ oz.) can cream of chicken soup
2 cups crumbled cornbread
Salt and pepper to taste

Chop onion and sauté lightly in margarine; mash up squash with fork. Combine onion and margarine mixture with slightly beaten eggs; add cream of chicken soup (undiluted), squash, cornbread, salt, and pepper. Mix well and pour into greased casserole. Bake at 350° for 20 to 25 minutes. Yields 6 servings.

Millie Allen

Pickled Beets

1 15 oz. can sliced beets
1/3-cup sugar
1/3 cup white vinegar
Dash of black pepper, to taste

Pour beets into a saucepan; add vinegar, sugar and pepper. Stir until sugar is dissolved. Cook beets with a slow boil about 10 minutes. Cool before serving. These will keep in the refrigerator a month. It is easy to double the recipe.

Cack Meyer

Black-Eyed Peas

2 cups dried black-eyed peas
Salt and pepper to taste
1 tablespoon bacon grease
¼ tsp. cayenne pepper
            or 1 small pod of hot pepper for extra seasoning, optional

Soak peas in water to cover for 6 to 8 hours or overnight. Drain. Cover with fresh water and cook until peas are soft. Season with salt, pepper, and bacon grease. Add pepper if desired.

Jean Weatherly

Main Dishes

Granddaddy's Spaghetti Sauce

1 lb. ground beef
2 cups tomatoes
8 oz. tomato sauce
½ cup chopped onions
½ cup bell pepper, chopped
1 teaspoon chili powder
1 teaspoon salt
1 tablespoon Worcestershire sauce

Brown beef and drain off grease. Add all other ingredients. Mix well and let simmer for 1 hour. Serve over spaghetti.

Mitsi Meyer

Porky Pines

1 lb. ground beef
¼ cup raw rice
1 medium onion, chopped
Salt and pepper to season
8 oz. can tomato sauce
¼ can water or more

Mix beef, rice, onion, and seasonings together; form into meatballs. Brown in skillet, drain and pat dry. Put into deep casserole dish. Mix tomato sauce and water and pour over meatballs. Cover and bake at 350° for 1 hour. All the Meyer boys love this dish!

Cack Meyer

Chinese Pork Chop Casserole

4 to 6 pork chops
Black pepper to taste
1 box long grain and wild rice
1 can cream of mushroom soup
1 can mixed Chinese vegetables

Pepper pork chops. Mix rice, soup and vegetable in casserole. Place chops on mixture. Bake 1-½ hours at 350°.

Mary Katherine Lawrence

Smoked Brisket

1 - 3 to 4 pound brisket
1 bottle liquid smoke
Garlic salt, to taste
Onion salt, to taste
Celery salt, to taste
Pepper, to taste
1 bottle Worcestershire sauce
1 bottle BBQ sauce of your choice

Trim visible fat from brisket. Sprinkle garlic salt, onion salt, celery salt and pepper over the meat. Place meat in baking dish. Pour liquid smoke over top, cover and refrigerate. Let meat marinate overnight . Try to turn the meat a couple of times while marinating. Before baking, pour on the bottle of Worcestershire sauce. Cover pan tightly with foil, and bake 5 hours at 300 degrees.
Pour BBQ sauce over meat and bake another hour. Pour off sauce; set aside to cool. Chill meat; then slice it across. Arrange slices in pan. Skim fat off cooled sauce; pour the sauce over meat, cover, and heat before serving.

Note: I do not bake my brisket the extra hour with the BBQ sauce added. I skim the fat from the juices in the pan, and add my BBQ sauce to those juices, making a combined sauce. Serve this sauce on the side.

Jennifer Cleary

Trippe's Favorite Ham Steaks

1 pkg. ham steaks
1 cup brown sugar
Prepared mustard

Cook ham steaks in skillet. Mix brown sugar and enough mustard to make a thick sauce. Pour mixture over ham steaks, heat, and serve.

Mitsi Meyer

Tater Tot® Casserole

1 lb. ground venison or beef
1/2 medium onion, chopped
1 can cream of mushroom soup
1 cube beef bouillon, dissolved in ¼ cup hot water
4 oz. Velveeta® cheese
1 pkg. frozen Tater Tots®

Brown meat and chopped onion in skillet. Drain if needed. Mix browned meat and onions with the bouillon and soup. Stir and place in a square casserole dish. Slice cheese and place a layer over the meat mixture. Top with an even layer of frozen Tater Tots. Salt and pepper potatoes to taste. Bake in 350° oven for 30 minutes or until bubbly. Serves 4-6.

Renelda Owen

Moo-Goo Lucy

1 medium onion, chopped
1 lb. hamburger meat
1 can whole tomatoes
Worcestershire sauce, lemon pepper, salt, black pepper,
    and garlic salt to taste
1 teaspoon chili powder
Flat egg noodles
Cheese
1 can cream of mushroom soup

Brown meat and onion together. Blend tomatoes until soupy and add to meat mixture; then add all seasonings to taste. Let cook 20 minutes covered. If this remains soupy, let it cook five minutes more, uncovered. Boil flat noodles according to package directions. Wash noodles and put in sauce. Add soup and mix well. Pour in casserole dish and top with shredded cheese. Bake until cheese is melted. (This recipe is from Lucille Magee who was Cack Meyer's housekeeper and nanny. She also helped take care of Cack's grandchildren.)

Karen Brunetti

Fratesi's Meat Balls with Lemon-Caper Sauce

1 lb. lean ground beef

1 cup seasoned breadcrumbs

½ medium diced onion

1 egg

1 teaspoon seasoning salt

1 teaspoon grated lemon rind

2 beef bouillon cubes

2 cups water

Combine meat, breadcrumbs, onion, egg, lemon rind and salt. Mix well. Shape into 12 meatballs. Bring water to a boil in saucepan. Add bouillon cubes. Stir until dissolved. Drop meatballs into liquid, reduce heat, and simmer for 8 to 10 minutes. Remove meatballs and keep warm while preparing sauce.

<u>Lemon-Caper Sauce</u>

1 cup of the bouillon mixture from cooking meatballs

1 tablespoon lemon juice

1 tablespoon cornstarch dissolved in 2 tablespoons cold water

1 egg yolk

2 tablespoons capers

Mix and pour over meatballs.

Mitsi Meyer

Soufflé Sandwich

"I first had this dish at the Woman's Exchange in Memphis. When Cack served it for lunch, Jim and Ed Meyer referred to it as "Soggy Bread," but it is good!"

8 trimmed slices white bread, buttered on both sides

Chopped ham for 4 sandwiches

4 slices Cheddar cheese

1 egg

2 cups milk

Salt and pepper to taste

A day ahead, make four sandwiches with the slices of buttered bread, the chopped ham, and the sliced cheese. (This is a good dish to make at the "end " of a baked ham.) Mix together the egg, milk, and salt and pepper. Fit sandwiches into an 8" x 8" square pan, buttered. Cover sandwiches with milk and egg mixture. Soak overnight. Bake uncovered in 400° for 45 minutes.

Editor's note: When this dish was brought to the Wednesday lunch, it caused quite a sensation and everyone begged for the recipe to be included in this collection.

Sue Latham

194

Paella

½ lb. shrimp, cleaned
2 cloves garlic, crushed
2 tablespoons butter or margarine
1 tablespoon cornstarch
1 ¼ cups chicken broth
1 can (14 ½ oz) stewed tomatoes with
    liquid
½ cup sliced pepperoni
1 10-oz. pkg. Birds Eye® peas, thawed
¼ teaspoon cayenne pepper
1 ½ cups dry Minute Rice®
1/8 teaspoon saffron (optional)

Sauté shrimp and garlic in butter until shrimp are pink. Stir in cornstarch and cook 1 minute. Add broth, tomatoes, pepperoni, vegetables, and cayenne pepper. Bring to a boil, stirring occasionally. Stir in rice and saffron. Cover. Remove from heat. Let stand five minutes. Fluff with a fork. (I add more shrimp and pepperoni, cayenne, and cocktail onions to suit my taste.)

Margaret Stevenson

Shrimp and Grits with Garlic and Lemon Zest

4 cups prepared grits
(yellow or white, seasoned to taste)
¾ cup whole milk or half and half
1/2 tsp. minced garlic (I like the kind in a jar)
1/2 tsp. salt
Zest of one lemon
1/2 cup lemon juice
1 lb. small cooked shrimp, peeled (I buy the frozen bags in the
    medium size that does not have the tails. If you like large ones,
    you can remove the tails when thawed.)

  Add to the cooked and seasoned grits ¾ cup whole milk or half and half. Stir to fluff. Sauté the shrimp in melted butter, garlic, salt, juice, and lemon zest until hot through and flavors blend. Stir into grits, reserving about ½ cup to garnish top. Add a dash of black pepper if desired.   You can also add Velveeta® or other cheeses to the grits if you like.   This keeps well in a Crock-pot® for buffet suppers, and will also reheat well. This works great adapted for a crowd. I have adapted this for over a hundred people and it is quick and affordable.

Renelda Owen

Fried Shrimp

Fresh shrimp, de-veined and peeled, split down back with knife
1 small can evaporated milk
2 eggs
1 tablespoon baking powder
2 tablespoons vinegar
Flour
Tony Chachere's Creole® Seasoning, to taste
Oil for frying

Mix milk, eggs, baking powder, and vinegar. Soak prepared shrimp in this mixture for 5 to 6 hours. Season flour with Creole seasoning to taste. Dip shrimp one at a time in flour; coat well and fry in hot oil. Delicious!

Karen Brunetti

Florentine Stuffed Fish

2 pkgs. 10 oz. frozen chopped spinach, thawed
2 cups sliced fresh mushrooms
3 tablespoons olive oil
1 cup ricotta cheese
1 egg, slightly beaten
1/3 cup herb seasoned stuffing mix
¼ cup grated Parmesan cheese
1 jar (2 oz) sliced pimiento, drained
½ teaspoon salt
½ teaspoon pepper
¼ teaspoon dried basil
1/8 teaspoon onion powder
2 lean fish fillets
Almandine butter (recipe follows)
Paprika

Drain thawed spinach in colander, pressing out excess moisture. Set aside. In 9 inch skillet, cook and stir mushroom in olive oil over medium heat until tender, about 4 min. Combine mushrooms, spinach, ricotta cheese, beaten egg, stuffing mix, Parmesan cheese, pimento, salt, pepper, basil and onion powder in medium bowl. Mix well. Set aside. Heat oven to 325°. Grease broiler pan. Place one fillet on pan, spread about half of the spinach stuffing on the fillet. Cut a slit lengthwise through middle of other fillet, leaving 3 inches uncut on each end. Place on top of spinach and other fillet. Spoon remaining spinach stuffing in the center of split fillet. Prepare Almandine butter, spoon half of buter over fish. Sprinkle with paprika, bake until both fillets flake easily at thickest part, 35 to 40 minutes. Serve with remaining butter.

<u>Almandine Butter</u>

1 teaspoon margarine or butter

¼ cup sliced almonds

5 tablespoons margarine or butter

1 tablespoon fresh lemon juice

Dash cayenne

½ cup butter

In small skillet, melt 1 tablespoon butter over medium heat. Add almonds. Cook and stir over medium heat until almonds are light brown, about 4 mins. Stir in 5 tablespoons butter, the lemon juice and cayenne. Cook over medium heat, stirring constantly until margarine melts.

Louise Meyer

Club House Barbecued Chicken

(Ed Garrison's recipe from MS Extension Service, used every year to make New Hope TCDC's famous barbecue chicken for their annual fund raiser and every time there was barbecued chicken around the Owen house.)

10 chicken halves

Salt

Sauce:

2 cups cider vinegar

1 cup vegetable oil

1 teaspoon Tabasco

½ teaspoon red pepper

½ teaspoon garlic powder

Prepare charcoal for grilling. (Old Diz® is preferred.) Coat all surfaces of chicken halves liberally with salt. (Much of it is removed in the mopping process.) Mix sauce and apply with a mop frequently during grilling. Place birds on grill and baste. Turn every ten to fifteen minutes, basting before and after each turn. Do not let chicken become dry at any time. Done when bone in leg will twist freely.

Rev. Billy N. Owen

Hot and Spicy Louisiana Chicken Wings

1 large package chicken wings
1 stick butter
1 bottle Louisiana hot sauce
1 package McCormick® original steak marinade

Cook wings in 325° oven for 30 minutes. Mix butter, hot sauce and marinade. Pour over wings and let marinate overnight. Remove from marinade and cook in oven for 1 ½ hours at 325° or cook on grill.

Virgie Jones "Tutter" White

Byerly's Chicken Wings

25 wings, cut in two
1 cup soy sauce
1 can chunk pineapple
1 ½ cups brown sugar
1 tablespoon Lea and Perrins® Worcestershire sauce
½ cup water
Minced garlic to taste

Place wings in 9 x 13 pan and bake 325° for 30 minutes. Mix ingredients and pour over wings after 30 minutes. Bake another hour. Leave in juice until ready to serve.

Virgie Jones "Tutter" White

Sunday Chicken

1 large fryer, split down the back
Salt and pepper to taste

Wash split fryer and let it drip. Salt and pepper it allover. Put in a large baking pan, skin side up. Bake for 10 minutes uncovered in a 500° oven. Remove from oven and cover chicken completely with foil. It is very important that the foil is air-tight on the pan. Turn oven down to 325° and cook for 2 ½ to 3 hours—until you get home from church.

Sue Latham

Chicken and Rice Casserole

2 cups cooked chicken, deboned

1 box long grain and wild rice

1 can cream of celery soup

1 cup mayonnaise

1 can French-style green beans

1 can water chestnuts, chopped

1 pkg. Pepperidge Farm® Stuffing Mix

Mix first six ingredients. Cover with stuffing mix. Bake at 350° until bubbly.

Mary Katherine Lawrence

Drunk Chicken

1- 3 to 4 lb. chicken

Lawry's Seasoned Salt

Tony Chachere's Cajun Seasoning®

1 12 oz. beer

Any barbecue seasonings, etc. that you like

Wash and drain chicken. Pat dry. Refrigerate until ready to cook on a charcoal grill. Put the coals, hot and glowing, toward the sides of the grill, leaving the middle of the grill open. Open the can of beer and pour out about ¼ cup. Remove the entire top of the can. Place the beer can into the rear of the chicken by carefully placing the chicken standing up on the can in the center of the grill. Be careful not to spill the beer. Cover the grill and cook for approximately 1-½ hours, rotating the chicken as necessary. The chicken is done when the juices run clear when pierced with a fork. Carefully remove the beer can from the chicken using mitts and discard the can. One chicken can serve 2 to 4, depending on appetites. (This is John Latham Meyer's recipe. In one of her cookbooks, Paula Deen of the Food Network calls this "Beer in the Rear.")

Sue Latham

Poppy Seed Chicken

Boil **4 large chicken breasts** with **salt, pepper,** some **celery and onion** for flavor for about 1 hour. Take chicken off the bone and cut into big chunks. Mix together **1 can of cream of mushroom soup and 1 cup sour cream**—stir into chicken pieces—put in greased casserole. Top with **1 "tube" of crushed Ritz Crackers®** and then pour **1 stick of melted oleo and 2 tablespoons poppy seed** over this. Bake uncovered in a 350° oven for about 20 –25 minutes.

Sue Rayner Latham

Chicken Spaghetti Casserole

4 whole chicken breasts
9 oz. thin spaghetti
3 to 4 stalks celery
1 small onion, chopped
1 bell pepper, chopped
2 cans cream of mushroom soup
2 cans sliced mushrooms, optional
1 lb. Mexican Velveeta® cheese
1 can Rotel® tomatoes
Parmesan cheese for topping

Boil chicken breasts and cut into bite size pieces. Boil spaghetti and set aside. Sauté onion, celery, bell pepper in butter. Add soup and mushrooms with juice and Rotel® tomatoes. Stir in Velveeta® cheese. Add cooked and drained spaghetti last, and stir all together until blended. Add salt and pepper to taste. Sprinkle top with Parmesan cheese. Put in casserole and bake at 350° until hot and bubbly. This freezes well.

Virgie Jones "Tutter" White

Dry Spice Rub for Chicken or Pork

3 tablespoons paprika
2 tablespoons seasoned salt
2 tablespoons garlic powder
2 tablespoons black pepper
1 teaspoon ground mustard
1 teaspoon oregano
1 teaspoon ground red pepper
½ teaspoon chili powder

Combine in a small mixing bowl. Makes about 6 ½ tablespoons of rub. Rub over meat. Cover and chill about 3 hours before cooking.

Mary Katherine Lawrence

Eggplant Parmesan

2 lbs. eggplant, peeled, and sliced ¼" to ½"

1 eggs, beaten

2 cups favorite spaghetti sauce (bought or homemade)

1 lb. shredded mozzarella cheese

Breadcrumbs, seasoned with Italian salt

Dip eggplant in egg, then in seasoned crumbs. Fry or bake until tender. Layer sauce, then eggplant slices, and cheese in casserole. Top with cheese. Bake at 350° for 30 to 40 minutes. Serve with salad and garlic bread. Voila—a wonderful meal!

Mary Katherine Lawrence

Roast Beef with Potatoes and Baby Carrots

3 to 4 lb. chuck roast (nicely marbled)

2 T. olive oil

4 ribs celery

6 to 8 potatoes, peeled and quartered

1 lb. baby carrots

1 medium onion, sliced or cut into strips

1 medium bell pepper, cored, and cut into strips

1 can golden mushroom soup

1 cup water or beef broth

1 pkg. dry onion soup mix

1 T. Zatarain's Creole® seasoning (or to taste)

Sear the chuck roast in the olive oil until browned on both sides. Place the celery ribs across the bottom of a large dark enamelware roaster. Place the meat on the celery ribs. (This works as a cooking rack with flavor.) Layer the raw vegetables over the meat. Sprinkle the dry mix and seasonings over the top and spread the soup and water over this. Cover with the roaster lid and bake at 350° for at least 2 hours. (Usually I start it at 400° and then lower the temperature to 300° and cook up to four hours, or to fit in with my schedule.) The lid keeps the natural juices in and allows for rich browning to occur. Allow to stand a few minutes, covered, before serving if possible. Serve with the *au jus* from the pan. This is the dish I brought to the potluck for the Smithsonian related Delta Bus Dinner Tour at Merigold.

Renelda Owen

Breads

Merigold Rolls/Bread

2 cups milk, scalded
½ cup sugar
3 heaping tablespoons Butter Crisco®
2 teaspoons salt

Scald milk and pour into your mixing bowl while hot. Add the sugar, salt, and Butter Crisco. Begin to mix slowly.

3 eggs
3 tsp. yeast
2 tablespoons sugar
Small amount very warm water

Beat eggs in a small bowl and set aside. Prepare yeast, sugar, and water. Let it begin to foam. Set aside.

7 cups plain flour

Dump 5 cups of the flour into your milk mixture and knead with mixer for approximately 5 minutes. Then add eggs and yeast mixture. Now, begin to slowly add the remaining two cups of flour. This is not exact. What I mean is, you may have to add a little more flour. You don't want a real thick/heavy dough. Knead this for another 5 minutes.

While kneading, grease a <u>large</u> bowl with Butter Crisco®. When the dough is ready, place it in the greased bowl and cover. Let this rise for about an hour.

I make my homemade bread, cinnamon rolls, smokies, and dinner rolls all from this recipe. The bread dough recipe makes 3 large or 4 medium loaves. The cinnamon roll recipe makes about 42 cinnamon rolls. The dinner roll recipe makes about 3-dozen rolls. I bake the bread at 350° for about 45 to 50 minutes. I bake the rolls at 375° for about 12 minutes. I bake the cinnamon rolls at 375° for about 18 minutes. Make a thin glaze and glaze the cinnamon rolls as soon as you take them out of the oven. Incidentally, all of the above freeze very well.

Virgie "Tutter" Jones White

Sallie's Rolls

1 cup water
¼ cup sugar
½ cup cooking oil
½ teaspoon salt
1 egg
1 package yeast

¼ cup lukewarm water with ½ teaspoon sugar

3 ½ cups all purpose flour

Bring 1 cup water to boil. Add oil, sugar and salt. Cook to lukewarm (100° to 140°). Beat egg. Dissolve yeast in the ¼ cup lukewarm water with ½ teaspoon sugar. Add egg and yeast to lukewarm mixture. Blend in flour until smooth. Cover with waxed paper and wet towel and refrigerate at least 4 hours. Turn out on a lightly floured surface. Knead lightly and roll to about 3/8-inch thickness. Cut with biscuit cutter and let rise about 1 hour. Bake at 400°. You may also choose to bake for only 8 minutes, and then cool and freeze for later baking. I use this same recipe for bread.

Mary Katherine Lawrence

Lucille Corn Bread

½ cup Martha White® self-rising corn meal

¼ cup Martha White® self-rising flour

½ teaspoon sugar

1 egg

1/3-cup milk

½ cup canola oil

1-tablespoon vegetable oil

Heat a 6-inch black iron skillet with 1-tablespoon oil. Heat until very hot. Beat all ingredients, as you would pancake mix. Pour into the hot skillet. Bake 20 minutes at 475° or until crusty brown.

Cack Meyer

Peach Bread

1 ½ sticks butter or margarine, softened

1 ½ cup sugar

5 small eggs

4 cups + 2 tablespoons flour

2 ¼ teaspoons baking powder

1 ½ teaspoon salt

¾ teaspoon soda

2 ¼ teaspoons cinnamon

3 cups sliced peaches

4 ½ tablespoons frozen orange juice
            concentrate (thawed, undiluted)

1 ½ teaspoons vanilla

Cream butter and sugar; add eggs one at a time. Combine next 5 ingredients; add to creamed mixture alternately with the peaches, beginning and ending with flour mixture. Stir in orange juice concentrate and vanilla. Pour batter into greased and floured pans. Bake at 350° for 1 hour. Test for doneness—may take longer. Cool in pan for 10 minutes; remove from pan and cool. Yields 2 9"x 5" loaves and 1 4"x 8" loaf or 48 regular size muffins.

Sue Latham

Strawberry Bread

2 cups whole strawberries
Sugar
3 cups + 2 tablespoons all-purpose flour
2 cups sugar
1-tablespoon cinnamon
1-teaspoon salt
1-teaspoon baking soda
1-¼ cups cooking oil
4 eggs, beaten
1 ¼ cup chopped pecans

Slice strawberries and place in a medium-size bowl. Sprinkle lightly with sugar and set aside while preparing bread. Preheat oven to 350°. Butter and flour pans. Combine flour, sugar, cinnamon, salt and baking soda in a large bowl and mix well. Blend oil and eggs into strawberries. Add to flour mixture. Stir in pecans, blending until dry ingredients are just moistened. Divide batter between pans. Bake loaves about 45 to 50 minutes, or until tester comes out clean. Let cool in pans on wire rack 10 minutes. Turn loaves out and cool completely. Yields 2 9"x 5" loaves, or 3 dozen muffins. Half this recipe to make 12 muffins and one small loaf.

Sue Latham

Sweets

Chocolate Cobbler

(This is similar to the one served at The Gallery in Merigold)

6 tablespoons butter
1-cup self-rising flour
1-¾ cups sugar, divided
1-½ tablespoons baking cocoa
½ cup milk
1-teaspoon vanilla
Additional ¼ cup cocoa
1-½ cups boiling water

Preheat oven to 350°. Melt butter in 9 x 13-inch pan. In a large bowl, mix together flour, ¾ cup sugar, and 1 ½ tablespoons cocoa. Add milk and vanilla. Spoon mixture into pan over melted butter; do not mix. Mix remaining 1-cup sugar and additional ¼ cup cocoa and sprinkle over other mixture; do not stir. Pour boiling water over top; do not mix. Make for 30 minutes. Serve warm, topped with ice cream.

Renelda Owen

Dranmomma's Cocoon Cookies

2 sticks butter
2 cups chopped pecans
¾ cup powdered sugar
2 ½ cups plain flour
Powdered sugar for dredging

Melt butter. Add sugar, flour, and nuts. This forms thick dough. Pinch off marble sized pieces and form into cocoon shapes. Bake very slowly in 300° to 325° oven until brown. While hot, roll in additional powdered sugar. John, Jason, and Edgar Meyer love these!

Sally Jo Lishman

Dot® Chocolate Cookies

6 Oz. Dot® Chocolate
1 can sweetened condensed milk
1 can (about 15 oz) of moist coconut
1 lump of butter, walnut sized
½ cup chopped pecans

Put chocolate in top of double boiler and cook until melted. Add condensed milk. Stir until mixed. Cook until thick (about 10 min.). Add butter, nuts, coconut and vanilla and stir again. Drop by teaspoon on buttered cookie sheet. Bake at 300° F for 12 minutes. Take up immediately. Put on cookie rack to cool.

Mary Aileen Lee Colucci from Aileen Ratliff Lee

Coconut-Orange Balls

12-oz. vanilla wafers, finely crushed
1 cup powdered sugar
1 cup coconut, shredded
1 cup pecans, finely chopped
1 6-oz. can orange juice concentrate

Roll into balls and then in more powdered sugar.

Renelda Owen

Oat Meal Ice Box Cookies

1 cup Crisco®
1 cup white sugar
1 cup brown sugar
2 eggs, beaten
1 ½ cups. flour
2 cups regular (not instant) oats
1 teaspoon. salt

1 teaspoon vanilla

1 cup chopped nuts

Cream shortening. Add sugar and eggs. Gradually add flour, vanilla, nuts and oatmeal. Bake about 10 min. at 300º F.

Mary Aileen Lee Colucci from Aileen Ratliff Lee

Ice Box Cookies

3 cups all purpose flour

1 cup brown sugar, firmly packed

½ teaspoon baking powder

1 cup. sugar

½ teaspoon baking soda

2 eggs

1 teaspoon salt

1 teaspoon vanilla

1 cup shortening

1 cup nuts, finely chopped

Sift flour, measure, resift three times with baking powder, soda and salt. Cream shortening with sugars thoroughly. Add eggs, vanilla and nuts and mix well. Add the flour mixture in 4 or 5 portions. Mix thoroughly after each addition. Divide the dough into 4 portions. Shape each portion in a roll 1 ¾" across. Wrap in wax paper. Chill several hours or overnight until dough is stiff enough to slice. Cut slices 3/8 in. thick. Bake on ungreased cookie sheet in moderate oven 375º about 12 minutes or until lightly browned. Remove from pan to cake rack. Makes 12 to 12 ½ dozen cookies.

Mary Aileen Lee Colucci from Aileen Ratliff Lee

Caramel Cookies

2 sticks margarine

2 cups dark brown sugar, packed

2 eggs

1 teaspoon vanilla

3 ½ cups plain flour

½ teaspoon salt

1 teaspoon baking soda

2 cups pecans, chopped

Mix margarine and dark brown sugar. Add eggs and beat. Add vanilla. Sift together flour, salt and soda. Mix flour into sugar mixture. This will be stiff. Stir in pecans. Using your hand, with waxed paper, roll the dough until a tight roll forms. Freeze. Slice and bake at 375° until brown, about 10 to 15 minutes.

Cack Meyer

Chocolate Oatmeal Cookies

2 cups sugar
½ cup margarine
½ cup milk
½ cup cocoa
Dash salt
2 tablespoon peanut butter
2 cups dry oats

Boil first 5 ingredients for two minutes, or until it reaches soft ball stage. Remove from heat and add oats and peanut butter. Stir and drop by spoonfuls onto waxed paper and allow to cool.

Renelda Owen

Caramel Graham Pecan Squares

Graham Crackers
2 sticks butter
1 cup packed brown sugar
1 teaspoon vanilla
1 ½ cups finely chopped pecans

Preheat oven to 350°. Lightly grease a jellyroll pan. Lay graham crackers to fill pan. Bring butter and brown sugar to a slow boil for about 2 minutes. Remove from heat and add vanilla and pecans. Pour over graham crackers and smooth out. Bake 10 minutes. While warm cut with a pizza cutter and go around edges to prevent tearing apart. Let cool and store in a tin to keep crisp and fresh.

Linda Hiter

Wren's Nests

3 cups Captain Crunch Peanut Butter® cereal
3 cups Rice Krispies®
2 cups roasted pecans
24 oz. white chocolate (almond bark)

Mix first 3 ingredients in large pan. Melt white chocolate and pour over the cereal and nuts mixture. Mix and toss. Drop by spoonfuls onto wax paper. Keep in tight container.

Renelda Owen

Fudge

2/3 cup cocoa
3 cups sugar
Dash salt
1 ½ cups milk

Combine ingredients and cook to the soft ball stage. Remove from heat. Add **1/4 cup butter** and **1 teaspoon vanilla**. Add **1 cup chopped pecans** if desired. Grease 9 x 11 pan lightly with butter. Pour fudge into pan and allow to set.

Monica Parker

Corn Flake Candy

4 cups corn flakes
1 cup peanut butter
⅔ cup white Karo syrup
⅔ cup sugar

Heat Karo and sugar. Remove from heat and stir in peanut butter. Pour mixture over corn flakes. Mix well and drop into generous portions on waxed paper.

You may also choose to form into loosely packed balls or clusters. Another variation is to add green food coloring to the mixture and form candy into wreaths or trees at Christmas.

Renelda Owen

Baked Custard

3 slightly beaten eggs
¾ cup sugar
Dash salt
3 cups milk, scalded
½ teaspoon vanilla
Nutmeg

Combine eggs, sugar, and salt; slowly add milk and vanilla. Pour into custard cups; sprinkle with nutmeg. Bake in a pan of hot water in 325° until "set", about 40 to 45 minutes. Serve warm or chill and serve. Makes about 10 cups (depending on size).

Sue Latham

Fresh Fruit with Custard Sauce

1 medium navel orange
3 egg yolks
3 tablespoons sugar
2 tablespoons heavy cream
3 cups fresh fruit, such as orange sections, fresh pineapple,
        kiwis, strawberries, pears, apples, melons, et cetera

Using a zester, remove zest from half the orange. In a small pan, boil ½ cup water and the orange zest for 30 seconds. Rinse zest under cold water and drain well. Squeeze juice

from the orange to measure ½ cup plus 1 teaspoon. In a small bowl set over a pan of simmering water (or double boiler) whisk together the egg yolks, sugar, orange juice and cream. Continue whisking over low heat until the mixture is frothy and thick enough to coat the back of a spoon (not long). Makes about ¾ cup. Arrange ¾ cup fruit in a dish. Spoon about 3 table-spoons sauce over each. Add orange zest to decorate. Sauce may be added warm or at room temperature. Zest may be added to the fruit or to the sauce or be sprinkled all over. I normally double this recipe because I use it a lot with company. It is really good after a heavy meal.

Virgie "Tutter" Jones White

Jason Meyer's Favorite Trifle

1 angel food cake
8 oz. cream cheese
2 small pkgs. vanilla instant pudding
2 cups powdered sugar
3 cups milk
2 cans peach *or* strawberry pie filling
Cool Whip

Tear cake into pieces. Mix sugar with cream cheese and mix milk with pudding. Add sugar mixture to pudding mixture. Layer in trifle dish alternately, the cake, the pudding mixture, and the pie filling. Top with Cool Whip®.

Karen Brunetti

Lemon-Layered Angel Food Cake

1 angel food cake

8 oz. Cool Whip®

1/3 cup lemon juice (I use bottled)

1 can sweetened-condensed milk

Make an angel food cake from a mix. You can do it—just like the box says! Split it into 3 layers horizontally, using a serrated or electric knife. Mix together the Cool Whip®, lemon juice, and condensed milk. Ice the cake between the layers and all around with this mixture. Make a day ahead and refrigerate. Mmm, good!

Sue Latham

John Latham Meyer's Favorite Butterfinger® Dessert

1 angel food cake

6 crushed Butterfinger® candy bars, blended well

1 large carton whipped topping

1 teaspoon vanilla

¼ cup butter, softened

2 cups confectioner's sugar

Mix sugar and butter well; add vanilla and stir into whipped topping. Break angel food cake into pieces. Layer crushed butterfingers and whipped topping mixture in trifle dish. Top with whipped topping and chill.

Karen Brunetti

Edgar Rayner Meyer's Favorite Chocolate Graham Layered Dessert

1 pkg. instant vanilla pudding and 2 cups milk,
prepared as directed

1 large container whipped topping

Honey Graham crackers

1 can chocolate cake frosting

Mix together the prepared pudding and whipped topping. Layer in the bottom of a 13" x 9" casserole the crackers and pudding mixture. Repeat layers and top with chocolate frosting that has been melted in the microwave. Chill and serve.

Karen Brunetti

Boston Cream Pie

(from Louise, one of the cooks at Flowers Manor)

1 layer of a yellow cake mix cake,
           prepared as directed (freeze other layer)
1 small box instant vanilla pudding
1/1 2 cups milk

Split cake layer. Mix pudding according to package directions, using only 1 ½ cups milk. After it "sets," spread between the layers. Pour chocolate icing over cake and chill well.

Chocolate Icing

3 tablespoons milk
2 tablespoons cocoa
¼ cup margarine
1 ½ cups confectioner's sugar

Boil together the milk, cocoa, and margarine. Add sugar. Pour over cake and spread.

Sue Latham

Chocolate Pie

1 baked pie shell
1/3 cup sifted flour
¼ teaspoon salt
4 tablespoons cocoa
2/3 cup sugar
2 cups scalded milk
3 egg yolks
1 teaspoon vanilla
2 tablespoons butter

Combine flour, salt, cocoa and sugar in top of double boiler. Add milk and cook until thick, stirring constantly in top of double boiler. Turn off heat long enough to stir in slightly beaten egg yolks. Stir and cook about 3 or 4 minutes, until quite thick. Remove from heat; add vanilla and butter. Cool. Pour into pie shell. Top with meringue. Brown in 325° oven.

Meringue

3 egg whites
6 tablespoons sugar
½ teaspoon vanilla

Beat until forms stiff peaks.

Sara Bess Meek

Coconut Cream Pie

1 cup sugar

5 tablespoons flour

3 egg yolks, well beaten

2 cups milk

1 tablespoon butter

1 teaspoon vanilla

1 cup coconut, with 2 tablespoons reserved

9-inch baked pie shell

Combine first three ingredients, and then add milk and butter. Cook over low heat, stirring until thick. Remove from heat and add vanilla and coconut. Pour into pie shell. Top with meringue.

Meringue

3 egg whites

6 tablespoons sugar

¼ teaspoon cream of tartar

1 teaspoon vanilla

Beat until stiff peaks form. Pour over pie. Sprinkle with reserved coconut and brown in 350 ° oven.

Karen Brunetti

Lemon-Coconut Pie

1 can lemon pie filling

1 cup sour cream

1 box coconut cream flavored instant pudding/pie filling

¾ cup milk

Mix all ingredients and pour into a **graham cracker crust**. Chill 15 minutes. Toast ¼ **cup coconut** and sprinkle on top.

Millie Allen

Key Lime Pie

1 can sweetened condensed milk

4 egg yolks

½ cup lime juice

4 egg whites

6 tablespoons sugar

½ teaspoon cream of tartar

1 baked pie shell

Mix first three ingredients. Beat 1 egg white stiff. Fold into mixture. Pour into pie shell. Beat 3 egg whites and gradually add sugar and cream of tartar. Top pie with this meringue mixture and bake at 350° until egg whites are golden brown.

Jean Weatherly

Pumpkin-Ice Cream Pie

1 quart vanilla ice cream, softened 1 hour

1 cup cooked or canned pumpkin

½ cup firmly packed brown sugar

1 teaspoon cinnamon

¼ teaspoon salt

¼ teaspoon nutmeg

¼ teaspoon cloves

Mix ingredients and pour into a pie shell. Freeze. This is good served with whipped topping.

Mary Katherine Lawrence

Strawberry Pie

1 baked pie shell

1 cup sugar

¼ cup corn starch

1/8 teaspoon salt

1 cup water

1/3 cup mashed strawberries

Red food coloring

Whole strawberries

Whipped topping

Mix sugar, cornstarch, salt, water, mashed strawberries and let cook until "starchy." Add food color as desired. Let cool. Arrange whole strawberries (you may cut in half) in baked pie shell. Pour mixture over berries. Chill. Serve with whipped topping.

Mary Katherine Lawrence

Nancy Lee's Vinegar Pie

(Everyone eagerly anticipates Nancy's bringing this on First Wednesdays)

1 pie crust, baked at 300° for 10 minutes

1 stick margarine, melted

1 ½ cups sugar

3 tablespoons flour

2 tablespoons white vinegar (I use Heinz®)

1 teaspoon vanilla

3 eggs

Mix pie filling ingredients and pour into baked crust. Cook at 300° for 35 to 40 minutes.

Nancy Seawright

Chess Pie

4 eggs
1 1/2 cups sugar
1/2 stick butter
1/4 cup milk
2 teaspoons corn meal
1 teaspoon lemon extract

Cream butter and sugar. Beat in eggs. Beat in remaining ingredients. Pour into pastry shell and bake at 300° for 45-50 minutes.

Monica Parker

Peggy's Pecan Pie

1/2 cup sugar
1/4 cup butter
1/4 cup white Karo®
3/4 cup red Karo®
1/4 teaspoon salt
3 eggs
1 teaspoon flour
1 cup chopped pecans
1 teaspoon vanilla

Cream butter and sugar. Add Karo®, flour and salt. Beat in eggs. Add pecans. Bake in pastry shell at 350° for 1 hour and 10 minutes.

Monica Parker

Heath Bar® Pie

1 large container Cool Whip®, thawed
1 cup Nestles Quik®
4 crushed Heath® bars
1 crushed Heath® bar for garnish
1 graham cracker pie crust

Mix first three ingredients together. Pour into graham cracker crust. Top with remaining candy. Let set at least 3 hours. Overnight is best.
*place candy in the freezer for 15 minutes to make crushing easier.

Jennifer Cleary

Apple Dumplings

2 Granny Smith apples
1 (8 ct.) package crescent dinner rolls
1 cup sugar
1 cup orange juice
1 stick butter or margarine
1 teaspoon cinnamon (or more, if you like)

Peel, core, and quarter apples. Roll each quarter in one crescent roll. Mix sugar, orange juice, melted margarine, and cinnamon. Pour over dumplings. Bake at approximately 350° for 20 minutes covered. Uncover and bake 20 minutes more. Watch carefully after uncovering, as they will start to brown. Brown to your preference for browned crust.

Sue Latham

Crown Pavlova

(from The Crown Restaurant in Indianola)

3 eggs whites at room temperature, beaten <u>very</u> stiff
1 cup sugar
2 teaspoons cornstarch

Mix sugar and cornstarch. Add slowly to egg white and whip. Then add **1teaspoon vinegar** and beat. Put into heavily buttered pie pan and bake at 325° for 30 minutes; turn oven to 200° and bake for 15 minutes. Let cool and remove from pan carefully.

Mix together **½ can chopped, drained apricots, and 8 oz. Cool Whip**. Put into piecrust and gently sprinkle a few **slivered almonds** over the top.

Virgie "Tutter" Jones White

Sue Latham's Tiger Cake

1 box yellow cake mix
1 cup water
1 cup oil
4 eggs
1 cup pecans
1 can coconut pecan frosting

Mix first four ingredients with electric mixer. Add pecans and frosting, mixing well. Put into greased Bundt® or tube pan. Bake at 350° for 1 hour. Check cake with a straw to see if done. Be careful not to overcook.

Nell Pitts

Buttermilk Pound Cake

1 cup butter

3 cups sugar

5 egg yolks

1/3 teaspoon soda

1 tablespoon hot water

1 cup buttermilk

3 cups flour

5 beaten egg whites

1 teaspoon vanilla

Cream butter, sugar, and egg yolks. Mix soda, ½ cup buttermilk, and water. Add this to creamed mixture. Add 3 cups flour and another ½ cup buttermilk. Fold in 5 beaten egg whites. Add 1 teaspoon vanilla. Bake at 325° for 1 hour. Don't peek.

Virgie "Tutter" Jones White

Buttermilk Cake or Muffins

1 cup + ¾ stick butter or margarine

(I use 1 stick butter and 1 ¾ sticks Imperial ® margarine)

3 cups sugar

6 eggs

3 cups sifted plain flour

¼ teaspoon salt

1 cup buttermilk

(You may substitute 1 ½ teaspoons white vinegar in 1 cup milk)

¼ teaspoon soda

1 teaspoon vanilla

Separate the eggs. Cream together well the butter and sugar; add the egg yolks. Mix flour and salt. Add ¾ cup of the buttermilk to the flour. Add ¼ teaspoon soda to the remaining ¼ cup buttermilk. Mix into the cake batter. Add vanilla. Fold in egg whites. Bake muffins in 375° oven until done. Bake cake in 300 ° oven for 1 ½ hours. Cut off heat for last 10 minutes of baking time for cake.

Sue Latham

Chocolate Cup Cakes

2 sticks butter

4 blocks dark chocolate

4 eggs

1 ½ cups sugar

1 cup flour

1 teaspoon vanilla

3 cups broken pecans

Melt butter with chocolate. Beat eggs and add sugar, flour, vanilla and pecans. Mix with butter and chocolate and pour into muffin tins lined with cupcake liners. Bake at 350°. Yields 24 cupcakes.

Mary Katherine Lawrence

Mamma Rosie's Sheath Cake

(One of Edgar Rayner Meyer's favorites)

2 cups sugar

2 cups plain flour

1 stick margarine

½ cup shortening

4 tablespoons cocoa

1 cup water

½ cup buttermilk

1 teaspoon soda

2 eggs

1 teaspoon vanilla

1 teaspoon cinnamon

Sift flour and sugar together in a large bowl. In a sauce pan, mix margarine, shortening, cocoa, and water. Bring to a rapid boil. Pour this mixture over the dry ingredients and stir well. Add buttermilk, soda, eggs, vanilla, and cinnamon. Mix well and pour into a greased pan at 400° for 20 to 25 minutes.

Icing

(Begin preparation 5 minutes before cake is done)

1 stick margarine

2 tablespoons cocoa

6 tablespoons milk

1 box confectioner's sugar

1 teaspoon vanilla

1 cup chopped pecans

Melt and bring to a boil the margarine, cocoa and milk. Remove from heat. Mix in sugar, vanilla, and pecans. Pour over hot cake. Let cool. Eat! Yum, yum!!

Karen Brunetti

Pear Preserve Cake

1 ½ cups sugar
2 cups flour
1-teaspoon soda
½ teaspoon salt
1-teaspoon cinnamon
1-teaspoon nutmeg
½ teaspoon allspice
½ teaspoon cloves
1cup vegetable oil
3 eggs
1cup buttermilk
1tablespoon vanilla
1pint pear preserves, processed with juice and all
1 cup chopped nuts
Buttermilk Glaze, optional

Combine dry ingredients in a large mixing bowl; add oil, beating well. Add eggs and beat well. Add buttermilk and vanilla, mixing thoroughly. Stir in preserves that have been ground in a food processor. (Divide before processing) Stir in pecans. Pour batter into a greased and floured 10" tube pan. Bake at 350° for 1 hour and 15 minutes. At this point, I pour the buttermilk glaze in the tube pan and let it soak into the cake. Turn out and let cool.

Buttermilk Glaze
¼ cup buttermilk
½ cup sugar
¼ teaspoon soda
1 ½ teaspoons corn starch
¼ cup margarine
1 teaspoon vanilla

Combine first 5 ingredients in saucepan; bring to a boil, and remove from heat. Stir in vanilla. Pour over hot cake.

Virgie "Tutter" Jones White

Blueberry Cream Cheese Pound Cake

1 box Duncan Golden Butter Recipe Cake mix

3 eggs

½ cup oil

8oz. cream cheese

15oz. blueberries

Drain blueberries well. Cut cream cheese into dry cake mix with two dinner knives. Beat eggs and add oil and mix well. Fold into cake mix until wet. Fold in blueberries and place in greased bundt pan. Bake 45 minutes at 350°.

Linda Hiter

Sue Latham's Chocolate Chip Pound Cake

1 box Duncan Hines® butter cake mix

1 4 oz. chocolate instant pudding mix

8 oz. sour cream

3 eggs

½ cup water

½ cup oil

1 6 oz/ pkg. Hershey® semisweet chocolate chips

Mix all ingredients together well, adding the chocolate chips last. Pour mixture in greased and floured Bundt® pan. Bake 1 hour at 300°.

Nell Pitts

Coonie Pound Cake

1 box Butter Duncan Hines® cake mix

½ stick butter

4 eggs

1 box French vanilla instant pudding

1 cup coconut

1 cup chopped pecans

½ cup oil

½ cup water

½ cup warm water

1 teaspoon vanilla flavoring

Mix and bake in Bundt® pan at 350° for 55 minutes.

Virgie "Tutter" Jones White

Pineapple Cake

1 box Pineapple Supreme cake mix
3/4 cup Crisco®
1 cup apricot nectar
4 eggs

Mix ingredients and bake in Bundt® pan for 1 hour at 350°.

<u>Icing</u>

1 cup sugar
1/2 cup milk

Mix over low heat until sugar is dissolved. Add **1 tablespoon butter** and **1/2 cup crushed drained pineapple**. Slice cake and pour icing onto cake while hot, separating sections.

Monica Parker

German Chocolate Cake

1 pkg. Baker's® German sweet chocolate
½ cup boiling water
1 cup butter
2 cups sugar
4 eggs, separated
1 teaspoon vanilla
½ teaspoon salt
1 teaspoon soda
2 ½ cups sifted cake flour
1 cup buttermilk

Melt chocolate in water; cool. Cream butter and sugar until light and fluffy; add egg yolks, one at a time, beating well after each addition. Add chocolate and vanilla, and mix well. In another bowl, sift together, salt, soda, and flour. Add this to butter and sugar mixture, alternating with the butter milk, beating until smooth after each addition.
In a small bowl, beat egg whites on high until stiff peaks form; gently fold this into batter. Pour into 3, 8 or 9-inch cake pans that have been lined with wax paper. Bake at 350 degrees for 35 to 40 minutes. Cool on racks about 10 minutes then remove from pans. Cool on racks for about 20 minutes, then frost.

Jennifer Cleary

Coconut Pecan Icing

1 ½ cups evaporated milk
1 ½ cups brown sugar
5 egg yolks
¾ cup butter
2 teaspoon vanilla
2 cups coconut
1 ½ cups chopped pecans

Combine milk, sugar, egg yolks, butter and vanilla in saucepan. Mix well. Cook over medium heat, stirring constantly until mixture thickens, about 12 minutes. Remove from heat; add coconut and pecans. This should be enough to frost entire cake (between layers, sides and top).

Jennifer Cleary

Sallie Lee's One Minute Chocolate Icing

1 stick margarine
2 cups sugar
2 tablespoons cocoa
½ cup milk

Bring the above to a boil and boil for 1 minute. Remove from heat and add **1 teaspoon vanilla**. Beat until right consistency to spread on cake.

Renelda Owen

Dot® Chocolate Candy

2 cups sugar
2 squares of Dot® chocolate
½ cup milk
½ cup nuts, chopped
Lump of butter the size of a walnut
1 tablespoon vanilla
1/3 cup white Karo®

Put sugar, Karo® and milk in heavy boiler. Let cook on high heat stirring a few times. Bring to a rolling boil. Let cook 1 min. on high. Then turn to medium heat and cook 4 !/2 minutes. Add butter and vanilla. Place in cold water and let stand about 15 minutes. Test to see if you can put your finger in and not burn it. Take the pan out of the water and beat the mixture a few strokes. Add nuts, stir in and pour in a greased pan. It will harden enough to cut in a few minutes. I put mine in a square pan and make 25 squares. If you stir the candy while cooking, it will be sugary.

Mary Aileen Lee Colucci (from Aileen Ratliff Lee)

Date Loaf Candy

2 cups. sugar
1 box pitted dates, chopped
1 cup milk
1 lump of butter, walnut sized
1 tablespoon Karo® (white)
1 cup chopped nuts
1 teaspoon. vanilla

Put sugar, milk, and Karo in a boiler. Boil until the soft ball stage is reached. Add dates and butter. Cook, stirring often until a ball is formed in cold water. Take off the heat and add the nuts and vanilla.

Mary Aileen Lee Colucci (from Aileen Ratliff Lee)

Divinity Candy

2 cups sugar
2 egg whites
½ cup water
1 teaspoon vanilla
½ cup white Karo® syrup

Heat sugar, water and Karo® in boiler. Stir constantly until sugar is dissolved. Continue to cook without stirring until the syrup makes a thread about 5 inches long or until 250° on a candy thermometer. Beat egg whites until stiff a few minutes before you take the candy from the stove. Pour the syrup a small stream at a time into the egg whites as you beat. Only pour up about half of the syrup at first. As the candy hardens, put the syrup back on the stove and cook just a few minutes. Then pour all the syrup at one time into the candy. I like to put my candy in the top of a double boiler over hot water. Keep beating until about ready to drop by teaspoon. I spoon my candy onto wax paper. Put in the vanilla after the candy comes off the fire. Add a pecan half or cherry on top of each piece of candy. This recipe makes about 30 pieces of candy.

Mary Aileen Lee Colucci (from Aileen Ratliff Lee)

Aileen Lee's Vanilla Ice Cream

6 eggs
1 quart milk
2 cups sugar
1 carton whipping cream
1 tablespoon flour
2 teaspoons vanilla, or to taste.

Beat eggs together with sugar and flour. Put milk on and cook on medium temperature until warm. Add the other ingredients, slowly stirring constantly. Add the cream, whipped lightly to the mixture after it is put in the ice cream freezer.

Mary Aileen Lee Colucci

Lotus Ice Cream

Hand squeezed juice from 8 oranges, 8 limes, 4 lemons
Pinch salt
½ cup crushed pineapple
2 ½ pints whipping cream
2 pints half and half
8 cups sugar
1 cup buttermilk
Whole milk

Mix together all the above ingredients except the whole mile. Pour into a a6 quart ice cream freezer. Add enough whole milk to finish filling the canister to fill line, if necessary. Makes 6 quarts. Do not use less sugar than called for. This is very rich and oh, so delicious. This came from Charley Dulaney and it is "beyond wonderful."

Sue Latham

Pickles and Preserves

Corinne Seawright's Chili Sauce

4 quarts peeled chopped tomatoes

2 cups chopped onion

1 cup sweet red pepper, chopped

1 cup chopped green pepper

1 small hot red pepper

3 tablespoons salt

½ cup sugar

1 teaspoon each of mustard seed, cinnamon, and All Spice

2 ½ cups vinegar

Combine vegetables, salt, and sugar. Cook until mixture thickens. Add vinegar and spices (in a bag). Cook until mixture becomes a thick sauce. Pour into hot jars. Seal immediately. Good!

Shirley Westerfield
Mary Katherine Lawrence

Dill Pickles

4 lbs. cucumbers

14 cloves garlic

6 tablespoons plain salt

3 cups vinegar

¾ cup dill seed

7 fresh heads of dill

21 peppercorns

3 cups water

Wash cucumbers. Slice in half lengthwise. Set aside. Peel garlic and slice in half. Add garlic to mixture of salt, vinegar, and water. Heat to boiling. Remove garlic and put 4 halves in clean hot jars. Add 2 tablespoons dill seed or 1 head of dill and 4 peppercorns in each jar. Pack with cucumbers. Fill each jar with boiling syrup up to ½ inch of top. Adjust lids and process in boiling water to cover for 10 minutes. Yields about 3 ½ to 4 quarts. *Note: We use cucumbers in fourths and soaked in lime water overnight, washed thoroughly, then in ice water the second night before pickling.*

Mary Katherine Lawrence

Mock Apple Rings

7 to 10 lbs. over ripe cucumbers, *peeled, seeded and*
    sliced crosswise into rings to result in 1 gallon of rings
1 cup pickling lime
Vinegar
6 cups sugar
1 bag Red Hots® cinnamon candies
8 sticks cinnamon
Water
1 tablespoon alum
¼ oz. red food coloring

<u>Step One:</u>   Mix 1 cup pickling lime with 1 gallon water and pour over rings; let stand 24 hours.

<u>Step Two:</u>   Remove rings and throw away lime water. Rinse well. Cover with ice water and soak three hours. Drain. Mix ½ cup vinegar, ¼ oz. bottle red food coloring 1 T. alum. Add rings and just enough water to cover; simmer 2 hours. Drain, and throw away juice.

<u>Step Three:</u>   Mix 2 ¼ cups water
        ¾ cups vinegar
        6 cups sugar
        8 sticks cinnamon
        1 bag Red Hots
Boil and pour over rings. Let stand 24 hours.

<u>Step Four:</u> Drain and reheat liquid. Let stand another 24 hours.

<u>Step Five:</u> Bring juice and rings to a boil. Pack in hot sterile jars and seal. Makes 8 to 9 pints.

Renelda Owen

Fig Preserves (Strawberry or Grape)

    3 ½ cups unpeeled figs, ground
    3 ½ cups sugar
    2 regular or 1 family size strawberry Jell-O®

Mix the above. Bring to a rolling boil. Boil for 3 minutes. Pour into sterilized jars immediately. Seal.

Pear Honey

3 quarts ground pears

5 lbs. sugar

3 lemons, cut into pieces, using rind

1 # 2 can crushed pineapple, <u>drained</u>

1 small jar maraschino cherries

Peel about 4 lbs. pears; put in food processor using steel blade, being careful not to over process. Drain pineapple well; add sugar to ground pears, and then add drained pineapple. Cook over low heat until it begins to simmer; then cook for 20 minutes, stirring frequently. About 5 minutes before it is ready to remove from the fire, add the lemons that have been cut into pieces (include rind) and the cherries that have been drained and cut into pieces. This will make about 16- ½ pint jars.

Molly Pemble Field,
via Bess Field Rayner,
via Sue Rayner Latham

Mother's Pear Relish

4 quarts ground pears

2 quarts ground onions

8 green sweet peppers

4 red sweet peppers

12 dill pickles

2 hot peppers

4 cups sugar

2 tablespoons turmeric

6 tablespoons dry mustard

8 tablespoons flour

2 quarts white vinegar

1 cup salt

Process the pears, onions, dill pickles, and peppers using the steel blade, being careful not to over process. I do this in small batches. Mix salt with this and let it drain a little before cooking. Mix the dry ingredients into a paste with a little vinegar. Add the rest of the vinegar—stir and boil for 5 minutes. You must really stir and watch this as it will stick and scorch very easily. Add pear mixture and boil for 3 minutes, stirring constantly. Seal in hot jars. Makes about 16 pints. This recipe can easily be halved. It is so good in stuffed eggs, potato salad, etc. It is not as much trouble as it may sound

Bess F. Rayner, *via* Sue Rayner Latham

For Further Reading

Edge, John T. *Southern Belly: The Ultimate Food Lover's Companion to the South*. Chapel

    Hill: Algonquin. 2007. Print.

Filippone, Peggy Trowbridge. *Home Cooking. About.com Guide. New York Times*.

    2010. Web. 16 Feb. 2010.

Hamilton, Mary. *Trials of the Earth: The Autobiograpphy of Mary Hamilton*. Helen Dick

    Davis, Ed. Jackson: UP of Mississippi, 1992. Print.

"Heirloom Weights and Measures Conversion Chart." *Home Cooking. About.com.*

    Guide. New York Times. 2010. Web. 16 Feb. 2010.

Oliver, Lynne. *Food Timeline.org*. 2000. Web. 16 Feb. 2010.

Sillers, Frances Warfield and Wirt A. Williams, Eds. *History of Bolivar County,*

    Mississippi. Cleveland: MS Delta Chapter DAR. 1948. Print.

Smith, Jimmy. *Merry Memories of Merigold, Mississippi*. Pittsburgh: RoseDog, 2005.

    Print.

Smithsonian Institution. *Key Ingredients: America By Food*. Smithsonian Institution

    Traveling Exhibition Service. N.d. Web. 16 Feb. 2010.

World War II Rationing. Ames Historical Society.org. 29 Jun. 2004. Web. 16 Feb.

    2010.

Index by Category

About the Author

    Renelda Owen teaches English at Delta State University in Cleveland, Mississippi. She is married to Rev. Billy N. Owen, pastor of Merigold and Cleveland First United Methodist Churches. She is the mother of two sons.

    She spent five years researching, compiling, and writing this book when she was not attending to her other duties. She has authored, served as editor, or served on the editorial staff of other cookbooks including *Worth Savoring: Literary, Visual, and Culinary Creations from the Hills of North Mississippi, Dinner on the Ground at Bethlehem, Feeding His Flock,* and *In the Kitchen with Delco.*

Made in the USA
Coppell, TX
26 July 2021